Living Stones

Pray Now Weekly Devotions
& Monthly Prayer Activities

Published on behalf of
THE PRAY NOW GROUP

SAINT ANDREW PRESS
Edinburgh

First published in 2015 by Saint Andrew Press
SAINT ANDREW PRESS
121 George Street
Edinburgh EH2 4YN

Second impression 2015

ISBN 978 0 86153 888 1

British Library Cataloguing in Publication Data
A catalogue record for this book is available from the British Library.

It is the publisher's policy to only use papers that are natural and recyclable and that have been manufactured from timber grown in renewable, properly managed forests. All of the manufacturing processes of the papers are expected to conform to the environmental regulations of the country of origin.

Typeset by Waverley Typesetters, Norfolk
Printed and bound in the United Kingdom by CPI Group (UK) Ltd

Contents

Preface

If the poet George Herbert was right to describe prayer as 'the Church's banquet', then this book will surely encourage us regularly to take our place at the table. Reading or hearing any of these fifty-two beautifully written meditations will lead naturally to prayer. Page by page, *Pray Now: Living Stones* offers us words of encouragement, inspiration and challenge in our walk with God.

One of the hallmarks of this book is its relevance to today's world. Through its chapters, echoes of some of the serious issues which nations, churches and individuals encounter week by week are brought into dialogue with readings from the Bible. Thus we are drawn into a deeper knowledge of God and of our own situations, leading us to 'something understood', another of George Herbert's descriptions of prayer. Enjoy the feast!

REV DAN CARMICHAEL
Vice-Convener, Resourcing Worship Team 2014,
Mission and Discipleship Council, Church of Scotland

Using this Book

*Come to him, a living stone, though rejected by mortals
yet chosen and precious in God's sight, and like living
stones, let yourselves be built into a spiritual house, to be
a holy priesthood, to offer spiritual sacrifices acceptable
to God through Jesus Christ.*

~ 1 Peter 2:4–5 ~

Living Stones is a prayer resource for use by everyone
across all denominations and none. The writers invite you
on a journey of discovery and reflection that you can follow
over any 52-week period or that you can simply dip into for
inspiration at any time.

For those readers who use the book at the time of first
publication and who are members of the Church of Scotland,
the *Living Stones* theme complements the Church's 'Heart
and Soul' year of celebration 2015–16. But this book is
an invaluable companion to your daily life, whatever your
denomination, if any, and in any year, in whatever month
you choose to begin to use it.

Living Stones prompts us all to meditate and pray about
our personal and communal response to God's love in our
daily living. Hopefully, the content of this book offers
comfort, reassurance, challenge and food for thought as well
as providing a structure for daily devotions and stimuli for
our own prayers.

Martin Luther said, 'To be a Christian without prayer, is
no more possible than to be alive without breathing.' This is
to suggest that prayer is a constant relationship and dialogue
with God either consciously or sub-consciously. Prayer takes
many forms, using silence, listening, speaking or completing

an action. Prayer can be guided or spontaneous. Prayer may be individual, shared with friends or family or as part of a communal act of worship.

Building on the history of the much-loved *Pray Now* series, the format of this book has evolved to take you through 52 weeks with a chapter for each, enabling the book to be used as both a weekly and a daily resource for prayer.

For the first two and final two weeks, we offer titles drawn from words used in our seminal text, I Peter 2:1–10. These are 'Chosen', 'Precious', 'A Royal Priesthood' and 'God's People' – each title relevant to our personal and communal relationship with God and our expression of discipleship.

The other weeks are made up of 16 titles, each related to 'stone' or 'stones' and each explored from three different perspectives:

- 'Landscape' reflects on how we view, take inspiration from, and interact with, natural stones and stone formations.
- 'Architecture' reflects on how, over the centuries, humanity has made use of stone to build, to trade, to create implements for good or evil and to commemorate people, places or events.
- 'People' reflects on the use of various stone metaphors to describe and represent the purpose, quality and characteristics of people with particular reference to those used in the Bible.

Each week offers the following:

- a Biblical verse that has stimulated the content for the week
- a short meditation
- a morning prayer
- an evening prayer
- two suggestions for Scriptural reading
- a blessing

Some users may wish to follow one title/week's complete programme of meditation and prayer daily for seven days, while others may wish to dip in and out of the content over the week, perhaps supplemented by some of the additional prayer activities at the end of the book.

There are 12 Prayer Activities shown at the end of the book, one of which may be used each month. These activities invite observation, self-awareness, self-appraisal, reflection, thanksgiving and praying for others. They invite us to explore our discipleship and mission and to reflect on how we make use of a variety of spaces to enable God to build us into a welcoming spiritual home for all ages and stages of faith.

Each Prayer Activity page may form a prayer project for a few weeks as the prayer activities both echo and also extend some of the titles in the 52 chapters. All activities lead with a classical or modern quote.

We have included blank spaces from time to time in the book on which you may wish to make your own prayer notes: thoughts that occur to you, a reminder, a form of diary or a quotation from the Bible or another source – maybe even something somebody said to you that day. Also, you could invite someone else to write something for you. This ensures that your copy of *Pray Now* will become unique – a 'Pray Wow'!

As well as for individual devotions, *Pray Now* may be used also by prayer groups or as a resource for reflective worship events.

However you choose to use *Pray Now*, the writers pray that your interaction with the book will enrich your journey of prayer and provide encouragement in your daily discipleship.

CAROL FORD
Convener of 'Pray Now' Writers Group
May 2015

For more information, the guide 'How to Pray' can be found on the Church of Scotland's Resourcing Mission website at: www.resourcingmission.org.uk/worship/prayer or phone 0131 225 5722 and ask to be put through to the Mission and Discipleship Council.

*Rid yourselves, therefore, of all malice, and all guile,
insincerity, envy, and all slander. Like newborn infants,
long for the pure, spiritual milk, so that by it you may grow
into salvation – if indeed you have tasted that the Lord is
good.*

*Come to him, a living stone, though rejected by mortals
yet chosen and precious in God's sight, and like living
stones,
let yourselves be built into a spiritual house,
to be a holy priesthood, to offer spiritual sacrifices
acceptable to God through Jesus Christ.
For it stands in scripture:
'See, I am laying in Zion a stone,
a cornerstone chosen and precious;
and whoever believes in him will not be put to shame.'
To you then who believe, he is precious;
but for those who do not believe,
'The stone that the builders rejected
has become the very head of the corner',
and
'A stone that makes them stumble,
and a rock that makes them fall.'
They stumble because they disobey the word,
as they were destined to do.*

*But you are a chosen race, a royal priesthood, a holy
nation,
God's own people, in order that you may proclaim
the mighty acts of him who called you out of darkness
into his marvellous light.
Once you were not a people,
but now you are God's people;
once you had not received mercy,
but now you have received mercy.*

~ 1 Peter 2:1–10 ~

Weeks of the Year

CHOSEN

Just as He chose us in Christ before the foundation
of the world to be holy and blameless before Him in love.

~ Ephesians 1:4 ~

Meditation

Chosen before time
as creation was crafted
constellations carved
earth formed
community shaped
covenant forged.

Called in old age
spoken to in dreams
summoned by fire
whispered to in a temple
hand-picked in youth
set apart in innocence.

Beckoned from a beach
taken from a tax desk
gathered from the edges
hauled from despair
lifted into relationship
bought for a price.

Chosen before and for all time,
a dream of the divine,
misfits and prophets
the raw and naive
the faithful and the fickle.
Love the only choice.

Morning Prayer

Here I am, Lord.
Is it I, Lord?
Am I the one You have chosen
to be Your messenger of love today?

To be the witness of Your grace?
To be Your hands and feet and voice
In a careless, stumbling, noisy world?
Do I have a choice?
I will go, Lord,
If You really need me
for I know that You hold me in Your heart.
AMEN

Evening Prayer

I have wept today, Lord,
for the dark places.
I have felt the pain, Lord,
of the hard places.
I have offered scraps of humanity, Lord,
in the hungry places.
And I give thanks, Lord,
That You sent me there
as Your light
as Your Word
as Your life.
Send me now, Lord,
the blessing of Your peace. AMEN

Scripture Readings

Ephesians 1:3–6   *Spiritual blessings in Christ*
John 15:16–17   *Bearing fruit*

Blessing

You are chosen,
choose peace.
You are chosen,
choose justice.
You are chosen,
choose life.

PRAYER NOTES

PRAYER NOTES

PRECIOUS

Because you are precious in my sight, and honoured,
and I love you, I give people in return for you,
nations in exchange for your life.

~ Isaiah 43:4 ~

Meditation

Precious –
For you are made in God's image.

Precious –
For you have the power to love.

Precious –
For you shine as a light in God's eyes.

Precious –
For you were bought with Christ's blood.

Precious –
For you are unique in this world.

Precious –
For you are a home for God's Spirit.

Precious –
For you have the ability to forgive.

Precious –
For you are loved and treasured by God.

Morning Prayer

Abundant God,
more precious than gold,
and far richer than rubies,
is Your eternal love.

You place true value in
whatever is good, and loving, and just,
and You encourage us to invest ourselves
into the wealth of Your economy.

Use us as Your currency in the world
that we might show something of Your lavishing grace
hallmarked upon our lives
and seen in all that we do. AMEN

Evening Prayer

We give thanks, O God,
that Your nature is Love.
Whenever we hurt You,
You forgive us.
Whenever we try to push You away
You reach out to draw us closer.
Whenever we forget You,
You remain by our side in readiness.
For Your capacity to love
is beyond measure.

Enfold us in Your Love
that we might find the strength
to love others,
as You love us. AMEN

Scripture Readings

Isaiah 43   *Restoration and protection promised*
Psalm 133   *Praise for unity*

Blessing

Never forget:
You are ...
adored,
cherished,
treasured,
by God. AMEN

PRAYER NOTES

PRAYER NOTES

FOUNDATIONS – *LANDSCAPE*

*He brought him outside and said, 'Look towards heaven
and count the stars, if you are able to count them.'
Then he said to him, 'So shall your descendants be.'*

~ Genesis 15:5 ~

Meditation

Glittering stones
studding the darkness;
the building bricks
of countless promises
prepared first
in heaven's landscape
and cemented in creation.
Each one a radiant truth
of a myriad mystery
which roots and raises us.
Each one a living reflection
of a rock-solid guarantee
that the groundwork
has just begun.

Morning Prayer

Night has passed
dawn has broken
light has come.
As sure as darkness slips quietly away,
as sure as stars make way for the sun,
as sure as life is birthed anew
beyond us and among us,
is Your love which underpins us.
May we begin this day, Lord,
firm in the belief
that we build on solid ground.
In Jesus' name. AMEN

Evening Prayer

Day has passed
dusk has fallen

darkness has come.
This day may or may not
have brought what we hoped for.
The building blocks of love and service
may have stood solidly or tumbled at our feet.
Your mystery may have enfolded us
or failed to touch us in our labours.
Thank You, all the same, Lord
for choosing and using us.
And may, in the darkness,
We keep our eyes fixed on the stars.
In Jesus' name. AMEN

Scripture readings

Genesis 1:14   *God creates the stars*
Isaiah 40:26   *The power of God in creation*

Blessing

May you count the stars
believing each is God's promise.
May each time you try
to catch the moon
remind you of God's mystery.
May each step you take
be as a brick laid in God's name.
And may His blessing
be embedded in your heart forever.

FOUNDATIONS – *ARCHITECTURE*

So Jacob rose early in the morning, and he took the stone that he had put under his head and set it up for a pillar and poured oil on the top of it. Then Jacob made a vow, saying, 'If God will be with me, and will keep me in this way that I go, … and this stone, which I have set up for a pillar, shall be God's house …'

~ Genesis 28:18, 20a, 22a ~

Meditation

Placed for a purpose;
to cushion the head
of a weary traveller;
to forge dreams
from the rubble of blessings;
to make stepping stones to heaven
in a holy place.

Placed for a purpose;
to carve sacred space
in a hostile land;
to be the signpost
of a promise fulfilled
and yet to come;
to be another brick in the house of God.

Morning Prayer

Today and every day, Lord,
we get a glimpse
of heaven touching earth.
It comes in the glory of dawn's kiss,
it thrives in the energy of life's landscape,
it grasps each glimpse of humanity within us.
May we learn to feel Your presence
graze our dreams and guide our visions
that we might know You are our God. AMEN

Evening Prayer

There is a time to build
And a time to pull down, Lord.

Forgive us for dismantling
the hopes and dreams of others.
Be with us when we search
for guidance and direction.
Help us to rest easy
with difficult choices.
Awaken us tomorrow
to fresh signs of Your presence
that we might be equipped and ready
to take them, and place them, with love.
AMEN

Scripture Readings

Genesis 28:10–22   *Jacob's dream at Bethel*
Luke 2:1–7   *The birth of Jesus*

Blessing

May God throw blessings
like pebbles in our way
that we might walk upon them,
gather them up
and carry them with us
wherever we go.
AMEN

FOUNDATIONS – *PEOPLE*

*They had been saying to one another, 'Who will roll away
the stone for us from the entrance to the tomb?'*

~ Mark 16:3 ~

Meditation

Just a stone
behind which a heart murmured
in the stillness of a tomb;
behind which blood coursed
through rigid limbs;
behind which life stirred
and graveclothes were strewn.

Just a stone
the first witness to a mystery;
the first to feel the breath of life;
the first to be touched
by the hand of God;
the first to be moved
by the Spirit's power.

Just a stone
rising and moving
to announce death was left behind;
before which men and women
stood in awe
as the emptiness
filled their souls with living.

Morning Prayer

Sometimes, Lord, it seems
my faith is mere gravel flying against the wind
of lovelessness and pain.
Yet You have chosen and placed me here;
laid Your grace deep within my being;
used my fragments in Your kingdom-building plan.
I pray, Lord, that today
even my shakiest stones

might be a safe place for others to tread.
In Jesus' name. AMEN

Evening Prayer

God at the root,
God at the centre,
God at the heart,
we give You thanks for
the day past,
the opportunities grasped,
the possibilities imagined;
for the living in Your love
the serving of Your people
the sharing of Your grace;
for making us Your own,
shaping us in faith,
sending us in service.
May we, Your stones,
forever cry out Your faithfulness. AMEN

Scripture Readings

Mark 16:1–7   *The Resurrection*
1 Corinthians 3:9b-17   *Servants of God*

Blessing

May we be anchored
as ancient standing stones
in God's grace.
May we be in life
the waymarkers of God's love.
May we be always moved
and always moving
in God's Spirit. AMEN

PRAYER NOTES

PRAYER NOTES

STANDING STONES – *LANDSCAPE*

*Those twelve stones, which they had taken out of the Jordan,
Joshua set up in Gilgal, saying to the Israelites, 'When your
children ask their parents in time to come, "What do these
stones mean" then you shall let your children know, "Israel
crossed over the Jordan here on dry ground."'*

~ Joshua 4:20–22 ~

Meditation

Mottled, grey soldiers of stone
stretch across the field.
Some erect and proud.
Some leaning jauntily,
offering a sign of unknown humour,
or a story never told,
while others have fallen,
collapsed with the weight of memory,
battered by the storms of anger,
and washed with the stains of dirt
flung by passers-by.

Like a caravan trail,
these markers in the ground
surround some hidden truth.
Lined in columns,
permanence and meaning combine,
and yet the reason is not always readily revealed.

A grassy canvas of a story
told through the strength
and time
of those who shaped and sculpted
with bone and wood.
In awe to the dawning day,
grasping at new understanding
of what it meant to be human,
stones aligned
with sun, moon and constellation.

When meaning cannot be easily grasped,
perhaps awe
opens the imagination.

Morning Prayer

God of the morning,
Your light dances around and between
the carefully placed
statues of wonder.
As the sun breaks on the day,
each shadow cast
points across the dewy grass
to highlight
that life begins
in the simplest form.
In the wonder of water
and mud
and clay,
may I sense the reshaping of my life
You will make this day.
AMEN

Evening Prayer

As the sun sets this evening,
Lord of rest,
help me to settle in Your presence
and recall this day.
Set out the markers
that will speak of You
and the invitation You have offered
to invest in Your love
and share it with those who encounter
the solidity of the standing stones
of faith.
AMEN

Scripture Readings

Joshua 4:14 -24   *Placing the markers for remembering*
Israel crossing the Jordan

Acts 17:22–31   *Paul in Athens at the stone of the unknown god*

Blessing

Bless us with the awe of spectacle
that unwittingly tells us of Your presence
even when we do not know Your name.
AMEN

STANDING STONES – *ARCHITECTURE*

*Then Noah built an altar to the Lord, and took of every clean
animal and of every clean bird, and offered
burnt-offerings on the altar.*

~ Genesis 8:20 ~

Meditation

Purposefully placed
by faithful, ancient people
searching for knowledge of the turning of day to night
and the rolling of the seasons,
or marking the passing
of warriors and chiels.[1]
A solitary stone stands with purpose,
connecting earth to heaven.
Gathered in a circle,
the fellowship of community
is embodied in rough-hewn stone.
Table-like,
the underside offers shelter
from the changing of time and weather.
The solidity of form
a clear indication of presence,
of the divine invitation
to express wonder and commitment to life
in earthly markers.

Morning Prayer

Ancient wonder,
standing proud
as a marker of the faith of generations past,
You call us towards You.
Intriguing us with Your antiquity,
we do not find You to be old.
Instead like the new day dawning,

---

[1] 'Chiels' is a Scots word which originally meant young man or woman or
child. In modern usage it is a generic term for 'people' used in the same
way as 'fellows'.

You bring the promise of yesterday
into the challenges of this day.
In the shifting patterns
of all that unfolds,
may the solidity of Your love
stand proud
in all we do.
AMEN

Evening Prayer

In the shadow of Your presence,
Stone of Ancient Hope
the world and all her cares
live, grow and die,
ebb and flow.
The cast of Your light
offers a place for reflection
on all that has happened
and all that is still to come.
While we know You to be unchanging
in the promise You have made,
as the waters of tears and frustration
erode the world's image of You
and as comfort and healing
smooth the corners of our gripes,
help us to encounter a new vision of Your hope
based on reflection of the place
and space
for wonder and worship
in community life.
AMEN

Scripture Readings

Genesis 8:15–22   *Noah and his family leave the ark*
Genesis 12:6–9   *The Lord's promise of land to Abram*

Blessing

Stone of the past
tell me the story.

Stone of the present,
shape me for this day.
Stone of the future,
call me in faith to serve.
Timeless presence
enfold me in Your time.
AMEN

STANDING STONES – *PEOPLE*

Now in Joppa there was a disciple whose name was Tabitha, which in Greek is Dorcas. She was devoted to good works and acts of charity.

~ Acts 9:36 ~

Meditation

The living of some lives
places a marker
in memory,
around which the past shared experience
can be explored,
or the future moulded
to enfold.
Figures of history,
prophets of change,
mark the past
with towering presence
that shadows
the Divine ambition
for hope and justice,
love and mercy.

Morning Prayer

Let us serve You with simplicity,
timeless Lord.
Strip back the face paint
and the bravado,
to the bare stone of who we are
beautifully created by You.
Let those we love
and those we meet
be the tools that shape us
to be Your people:
full of the hopes of those
who encouraged us to this day;
seeking Your justice
in the shadow of Your presence;
sharing love

when angry voices unsettle and hurt;
encountering mercy
as others offer the care and attention
of Your Kingdom. AMEN

Evening Prayer

God of all time,
thank You.
Thank You
for those who marked this day
with Your story.
Thank You
for those who have been
the markers in our lives
that point towards the wonder of You.
Thank You
for the steadfastness of others' faith
that has upheld
and lifted us
in times when we have felt laid low.
Thank You
for the stubborn stability
that has not shifted position
and therefore brought
compromise to bear.
In gratitude
we offer stones of story
that speak of faith. AMEN

Scripture Readings

Acts 9:36–42   *The healing of Dorcas*
Matthew 16:13–20   *Peter's declaration about Jesus*

Blessing

In the story of another,
may we meet You.
By the life of another,
may You shape us.
With the companionship of another,
may You guide us. AMEN

PRAYER NOTES

PRAYER NOTES

STEPPING STONES – *LANDSCAPE*

Then Elijah took his mantle and rolled it up, and struck the water; the water was parted to the one side and to the other, until the two of them crossed on dry ground.

~ 2 Kings 2:8 ~

Meditation

There they stand.
Sentinels to time and tide;
to guide my footsteps
and grant me passage
to the other side.

Up to their necks in water
to keep me warm and dry –
they must stand firm
when all around them moves;
they must resist the flow when the currents tug at their feet;
they must stay strong
when the hearts of wavering travellers doubt.

Theirs is the sacrifice to make,
Theirs is the load to bear,
Theirs is the time to endure.

And I in turn must put my trust in them.

Morning Prayer

When the day ahead seems full of uncertainty,
be the firm ground on which I can step, O God,
and the path to guide my feet.

Help me to put my trust in You
to guide,
and guard,
and grant me safe passage
as I walk through the waters of life.

When feet stumble
help me to regain my balance.
When legs are weary
help me to complete the journey.
And at the end of the day

let me rest in the knowledge
that You have been my travelling companion.
AMEN

Evening Prayer

Journeying God,
as the blanket of night encroaches
I give You thanks for this day past.
Bless those who have travelled beside me this day.
Bless those who have guided my steps
and given me direction.
Bless those who have helped me
on new pathways of discovery.
Bless those who have walked this path before me
and in whose footsteps I follow.
And help me, each and every day,
to be a blessing for those I travel with.

Companion God,
thank You for travelling by my side
in sunshine and in shadow,
up laborious climbs
and down descending slopes,
across rough ground
and along smooth plains.
And help me, each and every day,
to be mindful of You by my side.
AMEN

Scripture Readings

2 Kings 2:1–14   *Elijah and Elisha*
Psalm 121   *Assurance of God's Protection*

Blessing

Bless, O Lord,
the ground beneath my feet
the steps I take
the journeys I make
the thresholds I cross
and the people I meet.
AMEN

STEPPING STONES – *ARCHITECTURE*

And I tell you, you are Peter, and on this rock I will build
my church, and the gates of Hades will not prevail against it.

~ Matthew 16:18 ~

Meditation

As a babe in arms it embraced me,
as a child it taught me,
as a youth it inspired me,
as an adult it comforted me,
and in age it cared for me.

Like stepping stones in the stream of life
it has been present to help guide my steps
and be the rock on which to ground my faith.

Its strength and solidity
has allowed me to take the faltering steps of faith
in the knowledge of a secure footing beneath me.

It is Your rock,
Christ's body,
my stepping stone to faith,
our Church.

Morning Prayer

Lord God of light,
we give You thanks for the multi-coloured
community of faith
that we know as Your Church.

Bless us as we begin this day together
that throughout this day
You may inspire our thoughts,
enliven our conversations,
and stimulate our compassion.

Take us,
shape us,
make us,

into a truer image of Your Church here on earth,
that as living stones
we may support one another in our journeys of faith
and through the milestones of life.
AMEN

Evening Prayer

As shadows lengthen
and daylight dwindles
we give You thanks, O God, for this day.
For the glimpses of Your love
that we have seen, and shown,
in our striving to be Your Church.

Refresh our weary souls this night
that we may awaken renewed in faith
and strengthened to bear the weight of one another.

Help us to be stepping stones of faith
to all those we serve in Christ's name
helping to guide their steps
and bear their burdens.
AMEN

Scripture Readings

I Corinthians 3:10–15   *The Master Builder*
Matthew 16:13–20   *Peter's Declaration about Jesus*

Blessing

May the next step of faith
be always in your stride;
may the next leap of faith
be always from sure ground;
and as you cross the stepping stones of life
may God keep your soul balanced
and your feet dry.
AMEN

STEPPING STONES – *PEOPLE*

*Like living stones, let yourselves be built into a spiritual
house, to be a holy priesthood, to offer spiritual sacrifices
acceptable to God through Jesus Christ.*

~ 1 Peter 2:5 ~

Meditation

The stepping stones of life
are not measured by the ground beneath my feet,
but through
the love
and care
and nurture
of those who hold me in their thoughts
and treasure me in their hearts.

For they have been the ones
who fed me on my journey,
who helped me calibrate my compass,
who celebrated my every milestone,
who stood by me at every cross-road
and wait to welcome me home
at my journey's end.

Morning Prayer

Lord God of life, love, and relationships,
I give You thanks for all those who love me each day.
Their faith and love
flow through my blood.
Their hopes and pride
feed my dreams.
And their support
gives me strength.

Inspired by their, and Your, love for me
may I seek to be more
loving and forgiving
more gentle and generous
in all my relationships with others.

Throughout this day
may I seek to support and encourage
all those I meet
that they may walk sure footed beside me.
AMEN

Evening Prayer

God of sunset and curtain close,
of twilight and lamp light,
of tired minds and tired bodies.
This is a moment of rest before sleep;
a moment of thought before dreams;
a moment of prayer before pillows.

And in this moment I offer You:
the names of those I love
the places where healing is needed
the people whose lives are broken,
in the hope that tomorrow is a new day
and in the belief that step by step,
day by day,
Your Kingdom on earth is ever closer.
AMEN

Scripture Readings

I Peter 2:4–8   *Living stones*
2 Timothy 1:1–14   *Faith of our foremothers*

Blessing

Bless, O Lord, my soul
in every step I take
that I may tread lightly on life
and leave love's imprint in my wake.
AMEN

PRAYER NOTES

PRAYER NOTES

DRYSTANE DYKES – *LANDSCAPE*

God is our refuge and strength, a very present help in trouble.
Therefore we will not fear, though the earth should change,
though the mountains shake in the heart of the sea;
though its waters roar and foam, though the mountains
tremble with its tumult.

~ Psalm 46:1–3 ~

Meditation

Stones:
broken mountains, brought here aeons ago
by incredible, unimaginable forces,
by miles of ice, moving and moulding the land.
Stones:
buried deep in the ground,
never to be seen by human eye,
as we would bury the wrongs we do.
Or, brought to the surface by seismic action,
by upheaval and cataclysm,
exposed to scouring by wind and rain,
as our misdeeds come to light
and lie in plain sight
when our lying breaks down.
Stones:
ploughed up, or found,
long ago provided for the use
of builders of walls,
for partition and division,
for shelter and safety,
until this, our day.

Morning Prayer

Lord God,
in the morning of time You thought of us.
You ordered all things for our blessing,
including the ground under our feet.
In the morning of life You gave us breath,
You prepared a place for us to live,

to work, to enjoy.
In the morning of the day You rouse us,
You lift us, You hold out to us
the promise of new blessings.
Thank You, God, for the time ahead,
In Jesus' name. AMEN

Evening Prayer

You gave the day, Lord: we lived in it.
We made decisions, going this way or that;
we rushed; we had time on our hands;
we worried; we had fun;
we wept; we laughed.
Thank You for it all.
We place into Your protection
all those whom we love,
and ourselves.
Bless us and keep us, Lord,
all through the night.
In Jesus' name. AMEN

Scripture Readings

Genesis 1 *God the Maker of all*
Psalm 46 *God our Refuge*

Blessing

May God, the Lord of time,
be present in each of your moments.
May Christ's love and mercy
fill all your days.
May the Spirit bring you peace and joy
throughout your years,
in this life, and the life to come. AMEN

DRYSTANE DYKES – *ARCHITECTURE*

Then I said to them, 'You see the trouble we are in, how
Jerusalem lies in ruins with its gates burnt.
Come, let us rebuild the wall of Jerusalem,
so that we may no longer suffer disgrace.'

~ Nehemiah 2:17 ~

Meditation

They built to last, those who were before us.
Without mortar, they put stone on stone,
built walls, criss-crossing the land,
following the lines of the hills –
high up, then plunging down into the valleys.
Each stone lifted from the ground, or dug up,
by hands that weighed it, balanced it,
then placed it where it should go,
to lie there, day after day, year after year.

An ordered land, boundaries laid, patiently,
now to keep out raiders, protect the gathered flock;
now to keep the roaming sheep
from the dangers of the precipice.

Who were they that built dyke after dyke?
What were their thoughts as they handled the stones?
Did they think of those later-born, who would see
the marks of their labour
all over the face of the land?
Their work still stands,
a monument to their energy and skill.

Morning Prayer

God our Maker,
morning by morning new mercies I see,
given in blessing for this earth
and all who live in it
because You love us.
Help me not to take for granted
the abundance of Your providing.

In this new day, may Your hand guide me,
and Your joy empower me
for all the tasks ahead.
Your grace is indeed sufficient for me,
and I trust that Your strength will uphold me,
all the days of my life.
In Jesus' name I pray.
AMEN

Evening Prayer

Thank You, God, for the day just past.
My life may not be as ordered as I would like it to be,
but, in order or disorder, You are with me.
How many stones did I move today?
How many did I place, one on the other,
building walls around me, enclosing some
and keeping others out?
Did I act according to Your will, Lord?
Forgive me, Lord, where I did wrong,
and help me see more clearly
the way I should go.
Now quieten my mind
and still my heart, God,
for I am in need of rest.
I ask that through the night
You would enfold me
and refresh me,
and make me ready for another day.
In Jesus' name.
AMEN

Scripture Readings

Nehemiah 1 and 2	*Building and rebuilding a wall*
Mark 12:28–34	*Priorities in the Kingdom*

Blessing

Drop Thy still dews of quietness,
till all our strivings cease;
take from our souls the strain and stress,

and let our ordered lives confess
the beauty of Thy peace,
the beauty of Thy peace.

JOHN GREENLEAF WHITTIER

DRYSTANE DYKES – *PEOPLE*

You who live in the shelter of the Most High, who abide in the
shadow of the Almighty, will say to the Lord, 'My refuge and
my fortress; my God, in whom I trust.'

~ Psalm 91:1–2 ~

Meditation

There are those who stand firm
for generations,
like bulwarks around others,
shielding them, embracing them
with endless care.
No words are spoken,
yet they sense their neighbour's sorrow,
know something of their need,
their loneliness, their longing.
They respond in thoughtfulness,
quietly, the left hand
not knowing what the right is doing,
never looking to be repaid.

Deep within the structure of their being
live wisdom, steadfastness, compassion,
filling every space with love.
Each one a blessing
for us all.

Morning Prayer

Open my eyes to Your light, Holy One,
and let me recognise today
in the faces of others
Your own face.
Let me remember that all of us
are made in Your image,
that all of us need to be known
and loved.

At the start of the day I come to You
with my own emptiness,

with my hunger after You.
Fill me, Lord,
and I can be whole.
In Jesus' name. AMEN

Evening Prayer

So many people, Lord,
so many lives,
and I know so few.
Most of the time I'm overwhelmed
by what I see around me,
what I hear in the news,
and I find it hard to believe
that all will one day be well.
Lord, I pray for all those I met today,
some just in passing,
some face to face.
You know them all, Lord,
their sadness and their joy.
You know the things that worry them,
and those that make them glad.
Bless them Lord, as the sun goes down,
and surround them with walls of protection.
And, Lord, please also include me.
In Jesus' name. AMEN

Scripture Readings

Psalm 121	*Protection from God*
1 John 3:11–24	*Be there for one another*

Blessing

May the love of God surround you,
the peace of Christ enfold you,
and the compassion of the Holy Spirit sustain you
as you rest in the shelter of the Most High,
today, tomorrow, for ever. AMEN

PRAYER NOTES

DIVIDING WALLS – *LANDSCAPE*

For he is our peace; in his flesh he has made both groups into
one and has broken down the dividing wall, that is,
the hostility between us.

~ Ephesians 2:14 ~

Meditation

Stone after stone.
Carefully constructed
with the precision of the Romans.
A straight built line
that is curved by the landscape.

Moss and lichen disguise the chiselled hardness,
that tells us the people of the north,
must be separate from the people of the south.
That was the wall of Hadrian.

Slapdash breeze blocks
quickly thrown up.
Across 850 miles of land.
A wall of concrete imperfection.
Accentuated by barbed wire.

Tiny gaps in the mortar, offer a window of opportunity.
Lovers' names in graffiti disguise the hardness,
that tells us the people of the east,
must be separate from the people of the west.
That was the wall of Berlin.

How good we have become at building walls
from the days of Jericho to today in West Bank
we still find the reason to divide
and separate.

And yet we know,
that can't be Your way O God.
Can it?

Morning Prayer

I cannot tell what will happen today,
but I know that the lingering taste
of yesterday's pain
may shape me and my day.
Help me to do Your will
and build a house of peace
from the broken remains of the walls that divided yesterday.
AMEN

Evening Prayer

If I have built any walls today between others
or built a wall of seclusion from those I love,
then help me tear it down, God.
Forgive me for the moments when I have
sought to divide rather than unite
or widened the chasm of sin that separates me from You.
Help me to build new foundations tomorrow,
not division, bitterness or jealousy,
but love, joy and peace
AMEN

Scripture Readings

Ezekiel 13:10–16   *The wall is gone*
Isaiah 59   *Israel's confession of sins*

Blessing

May the stones indeed shout aloud.
May the voice of love, joy and peace
be yours this day and every day.
May the walls that separate us
fall quickly in the name of God's love.
May the God-given foundations of love, joy and peace
abound forevermore.

DIVIDING WALLS – *ARCHITECTURE*

Now the earth was corrupt in God's sight,
and the earth was filled with violence.

~ Genesis 6:11 ~

Meditation

B-14554
I pass through the iron gates
and I stand, pressing my back gently
against the barbed wire.
Until I feel the blood flow to the skin's surface
just like I used to do.
And the anaemic red brick
of the wall haunts me
still today.

The thin panes of glass
seem so clear today.
Clean, wiped of the iniquities of horror.
I press myself against the barbed wire.
Until the metallic thorn pierces my skin
and I feel the pain
of so long ago.

The wall of that building
was all that kept me alive.
It divided us, the survivors,
from those
who died
in the gas chamber.
B-14554
Arbeit Macht Frei Auschwitz.
Work will set you free.

Lies. Lies. Lies.
It was the dividing wall.
That set me free.

Morning Prayer

There is much that still haunts me.
The pain of the past is too much.
The anger of the present threatens to engulf me.
Forgive my wrongdoings
as I try to forgive those who did me wrong.
Teach me to truly understand forgiveness
and to embody grace and love.
AMEN

Evening Prayer

As I lay down this night
I lay down the complexities of the day.
I leave with You that which still troubles me.
I entrust to You my doubt and my longing to have faith,
knowing that all will be well
in Your sight.
AMEN

Scripture Readings

Psalm 139   *The depths of Sheol*
Joshua 6:20   *The collapse of the walls of Jericho*

Blessing

All shall be well, and all shall be well
and all manner of thing shall be well.

JULIAN OF NORWICH

DIVIDING WALLS – *PEOPLE*

Do two walk together unless they have made an appointment?

~ Amos 3:3 ~

Meditation

The walls are so thin,
woodchip and no insulation,
not built to last.
I can hear everything that goes on
on the other side.
The laughter, the hilarity,
conversations rising and falling,
the carefree clamour,
the clatter of cutlery
and the chink of glasses.
A land of milk and honey,
of tax avoidance and profit margins,
of Prosecco and Parma ham.

The walls are so thin,
woodchip and no insulation,
not built to last.
I wonder if they can hear me?
But what's the noise of hunger
or despair and fear of benefit cuts and arrears letters,
the rustle of the parcel from the foodbank
and the silent agony of having no electricity
to heat its contents.

I can hear everything.
Can they hear me?
Can they?
The walls are so thin,
woodchip and no insulation,
not built to last.
And yet, they still stand,
masking the hideous gulf between us.
Who's going to tear them down?

Morning Prayer

For those who will visit foodbanks today,
for those who will struggle to meet debt payments,
for those who cannot heat their homes,
for those who will rise hungry,
and for those whose bed was a doorway,
we offer these our prayers
that today might be a better day.
AMEN

Evening Prayer

For those whose bellies will be full tonight,
for those who will sleep easy,
for those whose life is well balanced,
for those with a portfolio,
and for those who snuggle into the eiderdown of plenty,
we offer these our prayers
that tomorrow might bring a sense of thanksgiving
and an understanding of those less fortunate.
AMEN

Scripture Readings

Deuteronomy 15:7–8   *Generosity to others*
Luke 4:18–19   *Good news to the poor*

Blessing

Above all things, know that God loves you,
in all that you are and all that you do,
and may the blessing of God Almighty be upon you,
and all those whom you love, forevermore.
AMEN

PRAYER NOTES

PRAYER NOTES

SAND – LANDSCAPE

*Therefore from one person, and this one as good as dead,
descendants were born, 'as many as the stars of heaven and as
the innumerable grains of sand by the seashore.'*

~ Hebrews 11:12 ~

Meditation

Seven billion people inhabit the earth.
Seven billion!
That is a number so large,
I struggle even to use figures
and instead resort to writing words.
A number so large
I cannot work out how many noughts
should be on the page.
A number so large
I struggle to think
how so many people can find their feet
upon the land that makes the earth.
A growing number,
as creation continues
to add to the wonder of God's world.

Humanity as innumerable
as grains of sand upon the beach.
From space the view suggests
the almost insignificance
of existence.
Such tiny specks
and yet capable of transforming.
Like sand,
humanity rubs along the shore line of history
and erodes the dominant features
of a generation.
Some of those changes are for the good,
allowing new light to shine,
or fresh water to plunge through to create new growth.
While at times
erosion leads to danger,

and life can crash upon the rocks
or fall into the sea.

Innumerable though we are,
it is the interest of God
that stirs the settled shores
of faith
causing the ripples
that lead to new visions
of the coastline of heaven.

Morning Prayer

Awakening Lord,
This morning I rise
and my mind is full of the thoughts
of the tasks that must be done today.
In the lists in my head,
I cannot see the spaces for reflection,
or times for silence.

In Your hands I place this day,
so that I might hear Your voice
and the intention of Your creation.
Through the innumerable cares and worries
may Your presence lead.
In the encounters with others
may You shape and smooth
Your creation,
so that our lists of impossible tasks
give way to signs of the wonder and purpose
of Your Kingdom. AMEN

Evening Prayer

From the business of each day,
Creator God,
You invite us to rest in Your embrace.
When the noise and tumult
of the storm of life
deafens us to Your call.
As You wash over us,
like the sea upon the beach,

You are not just relaxing us and settling us,
instead You shift our position in the shoreline
and re-energise us for Your purpose.
In the waking of tomorrow,
give us renewed vision
that allows Your justice and mercy
to ripple from the shoreline
into all of life. AMEN

Scripture Readings

Hebrews 11:1–16   *Faith of Ancestors*
2 Timothy 1:3–7   *Paul writes about Timothy's mother and grandmother*

Blessing

Water of God,
straying across the shoreline,
settle me in Your love,
wash me in Your hope,
and allow the ripple of Your mercy
to speak of You in life.
AMEN

SAND – *ARCHITECTURE*

*And everyone who hears these words of mine and does not act
on them will be like a foolish man who built his house on sand.
The rain fell, and the floods came, and the winds blew and beat
against that house, and it fell – and great was its fall!*

~ Matthew 7:26–27 ~

Meditation

It was a hot day
and after several weeks
of being there for others,
Jesus and his disciples decided to take some time out
and spend a day upon the beach
reflecting on all that had happened,
all that was around,
and all that was still to come.
Lifting the hems of their robes,
they paddled in the sea,
enjoying the coolness of the water on their toes.
Sitting,
sometimes in conversation
at other times in silence,
they built castles from the sand,
each reflecting the different personalities
of the group.
Some were covered in shells,
others had found feathers for flags,
others still had moats
to allow the sea to settle around the walls.

As the day drew to a close,
the tide scurried across the shore
and the work of the day
was destroyed,
returned to the rugged landscape of the shore,
and all journeyed on to the wisdom
of another day.

Of course it's not a story in the Gospels,
although we will encounter Jesus and the disciples

at work and rest.
In the parables
we meet the humanity of Jesus
relating the ordinary activities of life,
linking the encounters of faith, wisdom and folly.
For sandcastle building may not build permanent structures
on the shoreline,
but the experience of building and decay
may well change the pattern of living.

Morning Prayer

Architect of Creation,
who casts designs of beauty
across the sky, sea and shore,
we rise to praise You
for the wonder of this new day.
In all that we might build this day,
may we enjoy the process
of working with others and alone.
May our eyes enjoy
the colour and pattern,
our hands enjoy
the texture, strength and fragility,
and our ears
capture the sound and silence
of passing time.
As we allow You to create
Your Kingdom in all life,
may we stand upon the foundation
of the wisdom of Christ
and establish an organic community
that responds to the needs of the world.
AMEN

Evening Prayer

With the tides of life
You change the shoreline of our existence.
We thank You
for all that You have shown us this day

and all we have built in our activity.
Teach us to not be precious about
what we have done
and all we have achieved.
Instead may we lay our lives
at Your call,
so that the folly of our invention can be washed away
and instead leave standing the wisdom of shared living.
AMEN

Scripture Readings

Matthew 7:24–29   *Wise and Foolish Builders*
Proverbs 22:17–23   *Sayings of the Wise*

Blessing

Lord,
in Your wisdom
may You shape the sand of my life
to offer signs of Your presence.
AMEN

SAND – *PEOPLE*

*And of Zebulun he said: Rejoice, Zebulun, in your going out;
and Issachar, in your tents. They call peoples to the mountain;
there they offer the right sacrifices; for they suck the
affluence of the seas and the hidden treasures of the sand.*

~ Deuteronomy 33:18–19 ~

Meditation

If only every human being came with a treasure map.
A diagram that led you
to the 'x'
that marked the spot,
and allowed the hidden treasure of each person
to pour forth
in all its glistening, golden wonder.
Hidden within the shifting sands
of humanity
are sparkling gifts and talents,
all worthy of a place
within the tapestry of each day.

Morning Prayer

Lord of this new day,
You will embrace me
with the wonder of all that today will bring.
There will be old familiar patterns,
and new undiscovered ventures,
and in each of these
I place my hand in Yours
to be led to fresh discoveries.
When I choose
to focus on faces and opinions I trust,
encourage me
to listen for Your voice
in the discomfort of the unknown.
As the ripples of Your presence
push back the sands of what is known,
may the treasures of creation be revealed. AMEN

Evening Prayer

Lord of Revelation,
You surprise us with hidden treasures;
for behind haughty primness
kindness and welcome pour forth,
while masks of tattoos and piercings
cover interest and wisdom.
Forgive us for enjoying the simple pleasure
of the first encounter
or immediate impressions,
and encourage us
to dig a little deeper in the relationships
we build with You
and others.
AMEN

Scripture Readings

Deuteronomy 33:18–21	*Moses blesses the Tribe of Zebulun*
Philemon 1–21	*The Story of Onesimus*

Blessing

As the sands of life
ripple around our being,
may we be blessed
by the treasures that are revealed
when we push beyond the familiar
to the depths of Your presence.
AMEN

PRAYER NOTES

PRAYER NOTES

TABLETS OF STONE – *LANDSCAPE*

And in the seventh month, on the seventeenth day of the month, the ark came to rest on the mountains of Ararat.

~ Genesis 8:4 ~

Meditation

Did it leave an indelible mark?
There on the peak of Mount Ararat,
as it berthed on solid ground,
did the ark engrave the receiving rocks
with the marks of God's salvation?
We should not be surprised
that the Creator chose
the grandeur of a mountain plinth
on which to ground His covenant.
There was no writing –
just the tablet of stone
and the multi-coloured ink in the sky above,
speaking more
than words could ever say.

Morning Prayer

What is on the horizon for today, Lord?
Will I feel as if I'm at the top of the mountain,
secure in all my relationships,
my work and my ministering to others?
Or will this be a day when unexpectedly
I feel as if I am drowning in responsibilities,
expectations and misunderstandings?
Remind me Lord,
that I am grounded in Your blessing and promise
whatever the day may bring.
And if I need it, Lord,
please reassure me with a rainbow
smiling in the sky
or on the face of friend or stranger. AMEN

Evening Prayer

For what I have received today
and for what I have given:
thank You Lord.
Be with those who feel
they have received or given nothing –
the ones drowning in loneliness
the ones adrift from family or home,
the ones bereft of work or sense of purpose.
Redeem and heal
the ones who have had wicked thoughts
or done evil deeds
and the ones who have suffered at their
words or hands.
And bless all this day's many, many acts
of loving justice and kindness. AMEN

Scripture Readings

> Genesis 8:1–19   *The flood abates*
> Genesis 9:1–17   *God's covenant with Noah*

Blessing

> Wherever you spend the night:
> may the day's worries be put to rest
> may your body's burdens be relieved
> may God cradle you in his arms
> and breathe His peace and love
> deep into Your mind and heart. AMEN

TABLETS OF STONE – *ARCHITECTURE*

*When God finished speaking with Moses on Mount Sinai,
he gave him the two tablets of the covenant, tablets of stone,
written with the finger of God.*

~ Exodus 31:18 ~

Meditation

Set in tablets of stone
Your laws for living
defining,
binding,
reminding
Your people.

I can open my Bible now
and trace with my finger
those self-same words
that You wrote with Your finger.

But it isn't just the actions
of my finger
that define,
bind,
remind
me.

It is every part of me
that You command
to trace Your words
in relationship and action,
in life.

Morning Prayer

God in community,
today may I be faithful,
may I honour
those who love me most
and may I respond
with respect, honesty

and compassion
towards all the neighbours
I will meet –
the ones I expect to meet,
the familiar ones who will surprise me
and the ones who are as strangers
but to whom I have a duty of care. AMEN

Evening Prayer

Gracious God,
on those who today
have dishonoured their family,
stolen, lied or been jealous,
hurt, harmed or killed,
have mercy
and create a clean heart within them.
Compassionate God,
for those who today
have suffered through
the words or actions of others
bring healing to them
and to our communities. AMEN

Scripture Readings

Exodus 31:18 and 32:15–20 *The making and the breaking*

Exodus 34:1–10 *The remaking and renewing*

Blessing

May God
kiss the top of your head with His blessing,
consecrate your hands for His caring
cleanse your feet for His journeying
and fill you with love for His living. AMEN

TABLETS OF STONE – *PEOPLE*

And you show that you are a letter of Christ, prepared by us,
written not with ink but with the Spirit of the living God,
not on tablets of stone but on tablets of human hearts.

~ 2 Corinthians 3:3 ~

Meditation

Your law, O God,
not fixed to my doorpost,
nor tied to my wrist,
nor bound across my forehead
but within.
Your law inked
through my heart:
love You
love others.

Your law, O God,
living in Christ
now living in me.

Made in Your image, O God,
may the letters of my life
let others read:
'This copy is signed by the Author.'

Morning Prayer

Bless this day, O God,
those who are hungry and thirsty,
those who are strangers to their surroundings,
those who are homeless,
those who are ill
and those who are imprisoned.
And if in any way,
I can be part of Your answer
to my prayers for others
then may I be vigilant and ready
to fulfil Your purpose.

Evening Prayer

You have asked us
to live Your law to the letter
but I know I fall so short
of being the Christ to others.
So, forgive me, Lord,
for the times I was
less than hospitable
towards those
who needed my time,
my resources, my help, my company,
my love.
Break my heart anew
that I may be vulnerable
to the pain and needs of all
with whom I share this common life.
AMEN

Scripture Readings

Jeremiah 31:31–34 *The New Covenant*
2 Corinthians 3:1–18 *Ministers of the New Covenant*

Blessing

Christ be beside me
Christ be before me
Christ be behind me
Christ be within me
Christ be below me
Christ be above me
all of my days.
AMEN

PRAYER NOTES

PRAYER NOTES

TEMPLE – *LANDSCAPE*

Praise the Lord from the earth

~ Psalm 148:7a ~

Meditation

Sky my light
earth my mat
leaves my cushion
hills my altar
breeze my music
birds my choir
river my song
flowers my incense
roots my Bible
dew my cup
berries my bread
bower my shrine
stones my offering
silence Your grace
breath my salvation.

Everywhere
is a temple.

Morning Prayer

Let all creation praise You, Lord.
Let it sing and shout
in the world around me.
Let it breathe life and energy
into my day and dealings with others.
And if at all, Lord,
I should miss the glory that enfolds me,
fail to see I am
enclosed in Your power,
sheltered in Your mercy,
forgive me
and show me
the simplicity of the sacred. AMEN

Evening Prayer

Lord God,
sometimes my words
are like stones cast carelessly
in others' way.
Often I trample thoughtlessly
on the golden leaves of opportunity.
And now and then
my reason rushes and flashes
like a river in spate.
Thank You, Lord,
that, at the heart of my restless nature,
Your grace
refreshes and renews
the landscape of my soul.

Scripture Readings

Psalm 148   *A call for the universe to praise God*
Daniel 2:31–35   *Daniel explains his dream*

Blessing

May life's noise
be a gentle hymn to our hearts;
may the soul's silence
be our prayer for the world;
and may we, created,
be creative in our love.
AMEN

TEMPLE – *ARCHITECTURE*

As he came out of the temple, one of his disciples said to him,
'Look, Teacher, what large stones and what large buildings!'

~ Mark 13:1 ~

Meditation

A sacred place
is wonder-full.

Traces of the holy linger on walls
brushed by centuries of faith.
Prayers hide in the nooks and cracks
longing to be heard.
Hopes and dreams glide among the silence
echoing life.
Mystery smiles from the shadows
revealing glimpses of glory.
Stone speaks to smooth the edges
of the heart's roughness.

Buildings decline,
stones crumble,
fresh visions rise on consecrated ground
and we seek new temples.

Yet, touched by the divine,
sacred space
remains wonder-full.

Morning Prayer

Awake my soul, Lord,
for sometimes it slumbers
long beyond the alarm call.
The day is half done
before it stirs at the sight of You.
It is often short on awe
in the face of life's mundane.
And mystery passes it by
like the morning express.
Awake my soul, Lord,
that I may know wonder today. AMEN

Evening Prayer

It's no wonder, Lord,
that Your people are weary.
It's no wonder
that Your people are tired.
It's no wonder
that Your people ache.
Kingdom building
can be as fraught with danger and demands
as raising any temple.
As I toil, Lord,
remind me that glory comes
not in the ornate
but in the simple spaces in between
where grace is free to roam. AMEN

Scripture Readings

1 Kings 6	*Solomon builds the temple*
Mark 13:1–2	*Jesus speaks of the destruction of the Temple*

Blessing

Pride of man and earthly glory,
sword and crown betray His trust;
what with care and toil He buildeth,
tower and temple fall to dust.
But God's power, hour by hour,
is my temple and my tower.

All my hope on God is founded –
JOACHIM NEANDER (1650–1680);

translated from German to English
by ROBERT S. BRIDGES, 1899

TEMPLE – *PEOPLE*

My house shall be called a house of prayer;
but you are making it a den of robbers.

~ Matthew 21:13b ~

Meditation

It's turmoil inside.
Dirty dealings,
secret business,
trade-offs
for wrongdoings
and more confusion
than a flock of startled birds.
Then in comes
the uninvited guest,
up-ending fears,
freeing prayers
to flutter heavenward,
turning me around
to see the divine within.
And in my lameness
and my blindness
I am clean.

Morning Prayer

It may be
a little more shabby
than I would like.
It may have cracks
inside and out.
There may be dark corners
the light fails to reach.
Yet this body
is the only temple I have
with which to worship You, Lord.
I admit it's not always fit for purpose
and needs repairing from time to time.

Yet I ask that You receive it,
warts and all,
and that You stay.
For it is Yours. AMEN

Evening Prayer

All around me, Lord,
are walls
supporting the house in which I live,
surrounding the room in which I work,
sheltering the places where I walk.
And within me too, Lord,
are walls
shielding me from strangers,
containing my fears,
shoring up my inadequacies.
Lord, break down my defences,
make me derelict inside
and leave space
only for Your presence.
AMEN

Scripture Readings

Matthew 21:12–14   *Jesus cleanses the Temple*
1 Corinthians 6:19–20   *Use your body for God's glory*

Blessing

Strength in weakness,
freedom to fail,
softness in stone:
this, then, is the rock
of which the church is made.

Spoken Worship – Peter's Rock Song
GERARD KELLY

PRAYER NOTES

PRAYER NOTES

HOUSES – *LANDSCAPE*

From there he moved on to the hill country on the east of
Bethel, and pitched his tent, with Bethel on the west
and Ai on the east; and there he built an altar to the Lord
and invoked the name of the Lord. And Abram journeyed on
by stages toward the Negeb.

~ Genesis 12:8–9 ~

Meditation

So many of the stories of God's early followers
are stories of journeys,
of moving through the land,
of settling nowhere
and everywhere.
And when God sent Jesus,
He pitched his tent among us.
He did not build a temple.
He did not lay down stones.
He pitched his tent.

We are His travelling people,
moving through His travelling world,
watching the landscape change beside us –
the landscape
that we live in,
that He lives in,
living lightly,
moving slowly,
loving deeply.

Morning Prayer

Lord, You made this earth Your home.
You dwelt among us,
not as monarch,
but as neighbour.
When I move through the world today,
let me think of Your travelling feet,
beside mine.
Let me consider what it means to share this

home world
with You,
what it means to have Your tent
pitched beside mine. AMEN

Evening Prayer

Lord, as I fall asleep,
I think of those for whom
tented, travelling uncertainty
is not a liberation,
but an imprisonment.
As I lie down to rest,
I think of the tented cities of the world,
where children are born,
food is shared,
and fears are real.
I pray that You pitch Your tent among those people,
O Lord of travellers and refugees.
May they find comfort,
and safety,
and sleep. AMEN

Scripture Readings

Genesis 12:1–9   *The call of Abram*
1 John 1:1–18   *The word became flesh*

Blessing

God be in the going out and coming in of His people.
God be in the rocks of the foundations
and the fabric of the walls.
God be in our every movement through His world,
through His Word. AMEN

HOUSES – *ARCHITECTURE*

Unless the Lord builds the house,
those who build it labour in vain.
Unless the Lord guards the city,
the guard keeps watch in vain.
It is in vain that you rise up early
and go late to rest,
eating the bread of anxious toil;
for he gives sleep to his beloved.

~ Psalm 127:1–2 ~

Meditation

When I chose my home,
did I let God do the choosing?
When I made my home,
did I let God do the work?
Do I cling tight to my house,
or my flat or my room,
as if it is these four walls that protect me?
Or do I release it all
to the love of God?

Morning Prayer

Lord, as I prepare for the day,
I think through my plans,
the things I am worried about,
the things I am looking forward to.

I imagine You there already,
in my later-today,
and I know that when I arrive,
You will have prepared the way for me,
that You have made me feel at home
in the future You have planned.
Thank You, Lord,
for the home You make for me,
in every day and place.
AMEN

Evening Prayer

Lord as I relax after the day,
I reflect on all the homes that I have had.
I take a moment to think through each building,
the doors, the stairs, the walls,
the floors, the furniture.
Childhood homes I remember from photographs,
or other people's stories,
to the place where I live now.

Lord, bless my memories of those places,
and help me to see Your work,
and Your love,
in all the many homes of my life –
the homes that have been,
and the homes still to come.
Bless every one with the comfort
and challenge of You,
O Father Who is our home.

Scripture Readings

Psalm 127	*God's blessings in the home*
Proverbs 24:3–4	*A house is built by wisdom*

Blessing

The Lord bless the stones of your walls,
That they might protect you from the elements,
The Lord bless the stones of your doorways
That they might let in the love of friends.
And the Lord bless the stones of you,
That you may find a home with all people,
In Jesus' name.

HOUSES – *PEOPLE*

*But Mary treasured all these words
and pondered them in her heart.*

~ Luke 2:19 ~

Meditation

In the secret place of the womb
I was sheltered.
In the arms of friends, fathers,
mothers, grandparents, lovers,
I have been cradled.
In the hearts of strangers I have been
considered, pondered, protected.

God who shelters, and protects,
our certain help in trouble,
I think through all those
miraculous human acts,
by humans made in Your
miraculous image,
who have made
a home for my body,
who have cleared a safe place
for my soul to rest.

I will ponder them now.
Treasure them.
Make a home for them in my heart.

Morning Prayer

Dear Lord, our strength and refuge,
I give You thanks for the safe, human homes
You have given me here on earth.
Sometimes I feel that I move alone
through the world, exposed to the harsh weather
of the world's words.
Let me appreciate, today,
the people who have protected me,
who treasured me, who pondered me.

For hugs, kind words,
hand holding, hair stroking,
tear wiping, food sharing,
heart sharing,
I give You thanks, dear Lord,
knowing that every breath of the love I see and share
comes from Your perfect love,
that every moment of protection
is Your love in action.
AMEN

Evening Prayer

Give me strength, O Lord,
when I find that being a home for others
makes me vulnerable to having my soul
pierced too.
Mary pondered and treasured,
but also feared, and ached, and mourned.
Give me strength to know
that even when the wages of love are pain
love will triumph, that love is worth it,
that a home awaits me too,
in Your people and in my Creator.

Scripture Readings

Luke 2:15–51   *Mary's memories of Christ's childhood*
Mark 14:3–16   *Jesus discusses hospitality*

Blessing

May every blessing from my mouth
be as a comforting touch
on the bodies and souls
of the people You love. AMEN

PRAYER NOTES

PRAYER NOTES

STOREHOUSES – *LANDSCAPE*

He said, 'I heard the sound of you in the garden,
and I was afraid, because was naked; and I hid myself.'

~ Genesis 3:10 ~

Meditation

Walking deeply into the cave
I find dark corners, dank vaults,
shadowy recesses and clefts.
There I hide.
There I leave what I carry:
weights of worry, of sadness, of fear;
bundles of memories from times long gone;
a jumble of stuff that hinders, not helps,
none of it fit to be shared
with either friend or foe.

Who knows?
Left here in this hollow – maybe all will be forgotten,
never again to be brought out,
never again to be seen by human eye.

But, no matter how I struggle to store it all away,
it follows me and weighs me down.
Is there a place
for me to leave it all behind?

Morning Prayer

Mornings are hard, Lord God.
I open my eyes,
I come to,
and all the things I hoped would be gone,
lost in the depths of my sleep,
spill out again of their hiding places.
And again I'm overwhelmed,
troubled,
filled with anxiety.
Again I want to close my eyes and walk away.
I need Your help to face this day.

I pray for the courage
to take the steps I need to take,
and for the clarity to see priorities.
And help me to remember, Lord,
that everything can safely be left
in Your hands.
In Jesus' name I pray. AMEN

Evening Prayer

Thank You, God, for the promise of rest
as evening comes.
With Your help I've lived through another day.
And tonight I remember all those whose lives
are troubled in so many different ways:
those who have had to flee their homes,
leaving behind everything they know;
those who are in danger because of who they are;
those who have to face each day alone.
I lift them up to You
because You alone are the Lord of life.
In Your love and mercy, shield them,
and, from Your storehouse of blessings,
pour out on us all
the things of which we are needful,
for Jesus' sake. AMEN

Scripture Readings

     1 Kings 19   *Hiding in a cave*
     Ephesians 1   *God pours out his blessings*

Blessing

     May the Lord of all time
     lead you through each day,
     upholding you, and giving you strength
     to trust in His care.

STOREHOUSES – *ARCHITECTURE*

Consider the ravens: they neither sow nor reap,
they have neither storehouse nor barn, and yet God feeds them.
Of how much more value are you than the birds!

~ Luke 12:24 ~

Meditation

Gathering, storing, keeping things safe,
securing the future for us and ours.
Who did it first?
'This is mine, not yours,
and I need it for myself,
all of it.
Keep out!'

And so we accumulate,
we stack up stuff,
we store up possessions,
we fill our houses to overflowing
so that we can feel secure,
protected from what we fear
may lie over the horizon.

Often, though, our stores are full
and our hearts are empty.
All has been spent
on treasures that fail us,
that in the end leave us bereft.

Gathering, storing, keeping things safe,
securing the future for us and ours.
Most of us do it.
But real treasures come to us
through inviting
others in.

Morning Prayer

Keep me safe, Lord God,
keep me safe from myself

and the error of my ways.
My storehouse is full,
yet already I'm planning
to acquire more.
The protective wall around me
is gaining in height
as I add to it day by day.
Forgive me, God,
and help me to remember today
that You alone
are my rock and my protection,
and that without You
I can do nothing.
In Jesus' name I pray. AMEN

Evening Prayer

This night as every night
there are people
who go to bed hungry.
This night as every night
there are people
who go to bed troubled,
or lonely, or afraid.
This night as every night
there are people
whose sleep won't come for worry
about themselves
or those whom they love.
Some nights, Lord God,
I'm one of them.
Surround us all
with Your unfailing love,
and remind us again
that we are safe with You,
no matter what the morning will bring.
In Jesus' name. AMEN

Scripture Readings

| Luke 12:13–32 | *Rich towards God* |
| 2 Kings 20:1–21 | *Hezekiah's storehouses* |

Blessing

May God's presence
fill the longing in your heart;
may Christ's embrace
surround you with love;
may the Spirit's power
fill you with strength
for the living of this
and every day. AMEN

STOREHOUSES – *PEOPLE*

*By contrast, the fruit of the Spirit is love, joy, peace,
patience, kindness, generosity, faithfulness, gentleness,
and self-control. There is no law against such things.*

~ Galatians 5:22–23 ~

Meditation

I have known some,
those people who seem to be more real than others,
who lift the atmosphere in a room,
who make you want to sit at their feet
and hear them speak.

I have known some,
those people who are ready to listen,
who really hear you,
so you know you have been understood,
who make you want
to place your sadness into their hands.

I have known some,
those people who give of what they have
without counting the cost,
who are ready to help you find what you long for
deep inside,
who reach out, often unnoticed,
to those who are in need.

Their hearts are full of wisdom, of knowledge,
of compassion, of patience, of love,
like human storehouses from which they share
without bounds.

Morning Prayer

Lord God,
the bright morning has come again.
I thank You for the solace of sleep,
for the refreshment of rest,
and for the energy of expectation

as I look forward to what lies ahead
in the hours to come.
May the people I meet today
see in me one who has learnt
from my friendship with You
to share with others
Your gifts to me,
through Christ Jesus, Your Son,
and in his name. AMEN

Evening Prayer

Holy God,
You gave the day,
You filled it with good things,
You gave us community
to enjoy and celebrate.
We thank You for all Your gifts.
At this late hour I bring to You
all the people who are on my mind,
those whose names I know,
and those whose names I don't know,
and I ask that You would make
Your presence known to them,
tonight,
tomorrow,
according to their need.
And, Lord God, also keep me in Your love
as I lie down to sleep.
In Jesus' name. AMEN

Scripture Readings

Matthew 12:15–27   *Treasure of the heart*
Psalm 135   *God's storehouses*

Blessing

May you know the love of Christ
that surpasses knowledge,
so that you may be filled
with all the fullness of God. AMEN

PRAYER NOTES

MODERN ARCHITECTURE –
LANDSCAPE

*You are the light of the world. A city built on a hill
cannot be hidden. No one after lighting a lamp puts it under
the bushel basket, but on the lampstand,
and it gives light to all in the house.*

~ Matthew 5:14–15 ~

Meditation

Silver, glass and concrete,
scratching heaven.
Impossible metropolis,
made real in beautiful shapes and line.
A utopia of wealth, of growth, of hope.
But for so few.

High-rise flats on the horizon.
Concrete husks:
the chaff left behind
from the utopia that never came.
Beloved homes that hold memories of moments
and people
who love.

Concrete skeletons
sharp silhouettes against the sky.
Hardly a stone left.
Only air heavy with the dust of lives.
Place that violence-hollowed city
on the tallest mountain in the world –
you still could not make us see
what humans do to humans
in the darkness of war.

What is it that our cities say, from hill or valley?
What is it that we want them to proclaim to the world,
and to God?

Morning Prayer

As the light of day
descends into the cities of the world
may it illuminate the possibilities that modernity offers,
and show us how to use it
to help us love better.
May the light of today enlighten the lightness
of God's love
even in the heaviness of our cities.

Evening Prayer

Night-time cities are star-systems.
From space they spider out,
gold on black.
For You, God, there is no wide view
no panorama
there are only the people who live and work
in those single pools of night-time light.
Protect us with Your light
as we leave the day behind
and settle into the comfort and safety
and the darkness of sleep.

Scripture Readings

Matthew 5:14–16	*Light of the world*
Acts 17:13–17	*Paul travels to Athens*

Blessing

Lord, when I see images of cities,
new or old, growing or dying, vibrant or destroyed,
may You bless the people who live there
with the light of Your hope and love.

MODERN ARCHITECTURE –
ARCHITECTURE

Do not remember the former things, or consider the
things of old. I am about to do a new thing;
now it springs forth, do you not perceive it?
I will make a way in the wilderness and rivers in the desert.

~ Isaiah 43:18–19 ~

Meditation

Smooth lines.
Reflections.
Simplicity.
Light.

From the Gothic to the modern day
beautiful buildings have aspired to weightlessness,
to free themselves from the prosaic physics
of gravity –
struts
weights
measures
to look as light as air
to feel
divine,
to seem
new
to be seen
anew.

Morning Prayer

Newness doesn't always seem to be
a blessing, Lord.
New technology, new ideas,
even new days,
can all fill us with fear, with dread.
We feel comfortable
with the walls that we know –
even the structures that we hate
can seem soothingly familiar.

But we'd be better to rid ourselves of the devil we know
so we can open our doors to the newness
of You, Lord.

Let me be open to the good in the new today.
Let me see the beauty in transformation.
Let me seek out light, air,
the God in all things.

Evening Prayer

I reflect on the day, O Lord.
I think of the things I found hard.
I give to You the new things that frightened me
and the old things that I wanted to throw off.
Take these things, O Lord,
and mend me and them,
make us new.

Scripture Readings

Isaiah 43:18–19	*God names Himself*
2 Corinthians 5:16–21	*New life in the ministry of reconciliation*

Blessing

May each night of sleep renew my energy.
May each day of work renew my purpose.
May each person I meet renew my love.
May I feel Your blessing, new each day,
Lord, my father.

MODERN ARCHITECTURE – *PEOPLE*

Then I saw a new heaven and a new earth, for the first heaven
and the first earth had passed away, and the sea was no more.
And I saw the holy city, new Jerusalem, coming down out of
heaven from God, prepared as a bride adorned for her husband.

~ Revelation 21:1–2 ~

Meditation

The new earth is a city.
In the new earth,
buildings bubble up from the ground
to be filled with folk.
In the new earth the streets
are full of people,
people walking, driving, cycling,
going places,
hanging about,
partying, crying,
shouting, laughing,
shopping, talking.
The new earth is dressed up,
the new earth wants to celebrate
the love of God,
and the new earth wants to do it
in style.

Morning Prayer

Lord, it can be easy to find You
in the silence of a woodland,
or the stillness of a mountain
or the infinity of a sea.
But help me to find You today
in hustle and bustle,
in push and shove,
in busyness and craziness
in towns and cities.
You are in our land, O Lord,
but You are in our people.

Help me to love people
where they are today,
be it street, or shop,
or office, or hospital,
or home.

Evening Prayer

Lord, I will take a moment now
to consider some of the people
I encountered but did not speak to today –
whether on the bus, or at work,
or even on the TV or radio.

Lord, I pray that You be with them tonight,
wherever they are sleeping.
May they be filled by the joyful possibilities
of a new earth.
Amen

Scripture Readings

Revelation 21:1–5   *The new heaven and the new earth*
Jeremiah 29:4–7   *Jeremiah's letter to the exiles*

Blessing

Bless me in the city
and bless me in the country.
Bless me in the present
and bless me in the future.
Bless me in the busyness
and bless me in the calm,
O Lord of contrasts and continuity,
carry me through Your world.

PRAYER NOTES

PRAYER NOTES

ABANDONED BUILDINGS –
LANDSCAPE

*Is there any seed left in the barn? Do the vine, the fig tree,
the pomegranate, and the olive tree still yield nothing?
From this day on I will bless you.*

~ Haggai 2:19 ~

Meditation

The tree standing on
a burnt-out carpet
of brown, crackling leaves
teemed with life
only months ago:
squabbling magpies,
determined squirrels,
microscopic millions.

Today only wind and rain
rake among the branches
and fragile twigs
and it is not enough
to predict a new season
of growth and sunlight:
some future utopia.

It is now that counts
and now, in barrenness,
the idea of leaf
cannot be blown
from our mind's eye.

We are always more
than we seem, more
than we are made to feel.
Summer is rooted
in winter's shadow.

Morning Prayer

God of all time,
of past, present and future mornings;
before the day begins
You have been there.
With each memory
you shape me into
who I become tomorrow.
In the here and now
You call me
beyond myself
to Your unlimited
possibilities.
AMEN

Evening Prayer

By daylight we may have used
harsh words, spoken
when silence was best.
We have built ruins, husks,
and pray, by Your mercy,
for new growth, forgiveness,
wisdom in the dark.
AMEN

Scripture Readings

Haggai 2:15–19 *Blessings instead of Curses*
Matthew 21:18–22 *The Withered Fig Tree*

Blessing

From this day on,
from this unremarkable hour,
from this moment history
will not record,
God's blessing comes to you.
AMEN

ABANDONED BUILDINGS –
ARCHITECTURE

*Come, let us rebuild the wall of Jerusalem,
so that we may no longer suffer disgrace.*

~ Nehemiah 2:17b ~

Meditation

Where a roof was, rain
finds a path to pelt
the shattered glass on what
was once a floor.

An old plastic animal
gapes at a broken TV.
A donkey tries to force
a way through the rubble.

This was a house of worship,
play, bookcases, washing up.
This place, this plot, stirs
its memories like music.

Those who remember
still sing its song. And those
who listen find the song
burning in them like a fire.

Morning Prayer

God of holiness and wreckage,
I have risen from my bed
with only walls and ceilings
between me and the rubble
of world news: of war,
earthquake and flood.
They are like anguished
prayers howled from dust
and I, who am dust,
whisper in the early light.
Today, help me to treasure

acts of simple kindness;
help me to show love
to those who feel neglected,
betrayed or abandoned.
Help me not to tear down
but to build up. AMEN

Evening Prayer

For everything that erodes,
buffets and shatters;
for everything that aims
to break people's spirits
and destroy hope;
for everything that steals
power from the powerless,
hope from the hopeless,
love from the loveless;
Creator God, send forgiveness,
healing and wholeness. AMEN

Scripture Readings

Nehemiah 2:11–20 *Jerusalem in ruins*
John 2:13–21 *Jesus clears the Temple*

Blessing

Ancient psalms,
play Your melodies.
May Your words
live in my words;
may Your hope
furnish my hope;
may Your song
sing from my heart.
AMEN

ABANDONED BUILDINGS – *PEOPLE*

*Always carrying in the body the death of Jesus, so that
the life of Jesus may also be made visible in our bodies.
For while we live, we are always being given up to death for
Jesus' sake, so that the life of Jesus
may be made visible in our mortal flesh.*

~ 2 Corinthians 4:10–11 ~

Meditation

A church becomes a night club
or furniture salesroom.
What's the difference?

We fill ourselves with whatever
scraps we can find:
dance-high or perfect home
through which we twist
our mortal bodies.

We boogie in one shadow
of death or another.
We eke out personal hollows.

*My God, my God, why
have You forsaken me?*
We are dead stones
shouting aloud psalms
of protest and abandon.

But that voice shouting
is the death of Jesus,
so that His life may also
be seen in our bodies.

Morning Prayer

This is my morning hymn
rising like the first bird
to welcome the sky's
crisp, blue return.
I thank You for another
opportunity to live,

for everyone I love,
for everyone who loves me.
May the life of Jesus
fill me and every encounter
in the day ahead. AMEN

Evening Prayer

My evening hymn is spent.
It rose to darkness deeper
than the centre of a stone
and I am left with silence.

May its words and notes
endure like stars
when the blind sun rises
and they appear
to disappear. AMEN

Scripture Readings

2 Corinthians 4:6–12   *Life and death*
Psalm 22:1–11   *Trust in God*

Blessing

In the midst of life we are in death:
of whom may we seek for succour,
but of Thee, O Lord,
who for our sins art justly displeased?
Yet, O Lord God most holy,
O Lord most mighty,
O holy and most merciful Saviour,
deliver us not into the bitter pains of eternal death.

I am the resurrection and the life, saith the Lord:
he that believeth in me, though he were dead,
yet shall he live:
and whosoever liveth and believeth in me
shall never die.

from the *Book of Common Prayer, 1662*

PRAYER NOTES

PRAYER NOTES

BLOT ON THE LANDSCAPE –
LANDSCAPE

*For God so loved the world that he gave his only Son,
so that everyone who believes in him may not perish
but may have eternal life.*

~ John 3:16 ~

Meditation

Papers scattered,
food left half eaten,
homes left,
businesses abandoned,
streets emptied,
life left.

The screaming siren of meltdown
changed the landscape indelibly.
A mistake
of gargantuan proportion
but entirely of our own doing.

Life will never be the same again.
This is the point of no return.
This is the death of all that was familiar.

Suddenly the science of it all
is
utterly
irrelevant.
The tree of knowledge has died.

This is Chernobyl.

Morning Prayer

Forgiving God, You know us.
You know everything about us.
You know what we do
even before we imagine what we might do.

So You know that we make mistakes entirely of our own doing
day in, day out.

Forgive us for the things that we do
and the things that we will not do.

As we begin this day in prayer, give us clarity of mind, discernment of right and wrong and a resolve to do Your will.
AMEN

Evening Prayer

Hiroshima, Chernobyl,
indelible blots on the worldscape
that we cannot forget or fail to notice.
Help us in recognising the atrocity of massive disaster;
there are still the untold acts of destruction
that happen all around us.
You call us to be stewards of Your earth
yet we contribute daily to the murder of Your creation
through pollution,
wastefulness and corporate ignorance.
Open our eyes
to all that You have created
and wake us to the responsibility
we have to love and cherish You
and Your creation.
AMEN

Scripture Readings

| Genesis 2:17 | *The tree of life* |
| Colossians 3:2 | *Setting our minds on heavenly things* |

Blessing

Life ebbs and flows,
the beginning becomes the end,
the end becomes a new beginning.
May God bless us
in our coming and our going.

BLOT ON THE LANDSCAPE –
ARCHITECTURE

*And have them make me a sanctuary,
so that I may dwell among them.*

~ Exodus 25:8 ~

Meditation

They call it a carbuncle –
there's even an award for it.
Grey concrete box.
Rising damp and festering mould,
thirty-five floors high.
Swaying precariously in the cold east wind.
Their own people deserted long ago,
a slum, not fit for living in.
Ugly, grey concrete box.
But for me, life on the 22nd floor
is sanctuary, despite its apparent ugliness.

You see, it's not Rwanda
and I no longer have to run.
Thank God.

Morning Prayer

Let us look beyond the ugliness.
Take our thinking
outside
the grey concrete box,
to a place
where our eyes are opened
and we see the opportunity,
of freedom and love,
for those
who run from
violence
and
fear
to
sanctuary. AMEN

Evening Prayer

God of the night,
may this be
a safe passage
to daybreak.
May we hold in our hearts
those for whom the night is
cold and long.
May the warmth of Your love
be an all-embracing and encircling
sanctuary.
AMEN

Scripture Readings

Psalm 15:1–5	*Sojourners*
Philippians 3:20	*Citizenship in heaven*

Blessing

Amidst the rising damp and festering mould of life
may there be the warmth of light and love that is Yours, God.
A new dawn
A new day
A new place
And may we feel truly blessed.
AMEN

BLOT ON THE LANDSCAPE – *PEOPLE*

> *learn to do good; seek justice, rescue the oppressed,*
> *defend the orphan, plead for the widow.*

> ~ Isaiah 1:17 ~

Meditation

The Great War, Congo Free State,
World War Two, Vietnam,
Chairman Mao, Pol Pot, Ceausescu,
Stalin, Khmer Rouge,
Rwanda, Somalia,
Garvaghy Road,
Iran, Iraq,
Afghanistan.
History's shame:
the blot on the landscape
of our common lives
to name but a few.

Emmeline Pankhurst, Rosa Parks,
Winston Churchill, Nelson Mandela,
Yitzhak Rabin, Martin Luther King Jr,
Mahatma Ghandi, Mother Theresa,
Charles de Gaulle, Ralph Nader.
History's pride:
the beauty of the landscape
of our common lives
to name but a few.

Morning Prayer

As the sun rises out of the darkness
spilling light onto ripened grain,
so too must the joys of this earth shine bright,
sure that there is goodness
and love and forgiveness.
May we pray for all who try to make this world a better place
and may we catch a glimpse of heaven,
in serving Your Kingdom here on earth. AMEN

Evening Prayer

The sun sets, the light is extinguished.
The darkness looms and the shadows of evil lurk.
There is much still wrong with this world,
the shame of history is still here today.
Let us pray this night –
for those who are oppressed,
for victims of violence,
for women and children,
husbands and fathers and brothers in war-torn countries.
And for those who live in darkness much closer to home,
may the shard of light in the darkness of night,
be a glimpse of the dawn of Your Kingdom.
AMEN

Scripture Readings

Jeremiah 22:13–17   *Building with Righteousness*
Matthew 25:31–46   *Sheep and Goats*

Blessing

Guide the people of this land,
and of all the nations,
in the ways of justice and peace;
that we may honour one another
and serve the common good
surrounded by Your blessings and love.

PRAYER NOTES

PRAYER NOTES

WEAPONS – *LANDSCAPE*

*When they kept on questioning him, he straightened up
and said to them, 'Let anyone among you who is without sin
be the first to throw a stone at her.'*

~ John 8:7 ~

Meditation

The rain beats down:
a rain of shrapnel, bullets and bombs,
a rain of power and self-righteousness
from the kingdom of terror.

And the stones are aimed still
at this woman caught in adultery.

Was the man she slept with
in the crowd, his arm raised,
his fist tight around a rock?
Was he first or last to turn,
angry only at himself,
and walk away?

In the kingdom of terror,
stones ready themselves
to rain down like nails
on flesh, while in sand
Jesus draws a different way
with a fragile hand.

Morning Prayer

Keep me from speaking
when silence gives space to feel;
keep me from silence
when the unfeeling unfold
their flags of blood;
keep me from shouting
when challenged by a whisper;
keep me from judgement
when fact and emotion

are in dispute;
keep me from confusing
truth with popularity,
eloquence with persuasion;
keep me from loving more
the sound of my own voice
than the inexpressible mystery
of Yours.

Evening Prayer

Between the home and its ruin
   You live
Between the weaponry and casualty
   You grieve
Among the bruisers and the bruised
   You heal
Among the loveless and the lifeless
   You fill.

Scripture Readings

Isaiah 53:2–9   *The suffering servant*
John 8:1–9   *A woman sentenced to be stoned*

Blessing

May You who opened hands
to drop stones
and accept nails;
open our hands
as cradles for everything
You wish held in us. AMEN

WEAPONS – *ARCHITECTURE*

*Tobiah the Ammonite was beside him, and he said,
'That stone wall they are building – any fox going up
on it would break it down!'*

~ Nehemiah 4:3 ~

Meditation

She has spent years
shaping curious objects
from timber, wax and stone.

She exhibits them
on home-crafted pedestals
in tiny city galleries
and watches bodies
trudge by, weighed down
with shopping bags.

A few people drop in
to admire her work
or avoid the rain.
Others tell her
to get a real job,
that roofs are leaking,
new wars are beginning
and sculpture changes nothing.

Their words change nothing.
Her work keeps reshaping
the minds of the curious.

Morning Prayer

Give me strength;
not the guile of those
who outfox an opponent,
not the laughter of those
who knock over what others
have taken weeks to build.
Make me a rock
so that people may find
shelter from the darts,

refuge from the blows.
May they not overwhelm me. AMEN

Evening Prayer

I bring to You my parish,
community, street and home.
You know where the day began
with positive thoughts
that were mocked and belittled
and came to nothing.
You sense the disappointment,
the loss of an unrepeatable day.
Would I live today again
differently if I could?
The truth is, I always could.
Encourage all who build
in a cynical climate
where effort is scorned,
where 'it won't happen'
becomes a self-defeating truth.
May every small happening
become a counter-vision.
Give us new eyes.
AMEN

Scripture Readings

Nehemiah 4:1–9   *Opposition to the rebuilding*
Romans 12:1–13   *Using our gifts for God*

Blessing

May words I speak
and words I listen to
come subtle as a fox
or strong as a stone wall
and become Your blessing.
AMEN

WEAPONS – *PEOPLE*

See, I have made your face hard against their faces,
and your forehead hard against their foreheads. Like the
hardest stone, harder than flint, I have made your forehead;

~ Ezekiel 3:8–9a ~

Meditation

The Road from Emmaus

Didn't our hearts burn within us
while he talked with us on the road?

And suddenly as he came
he disappears

        leaving us

like timbers   glowing after conflagration
apt at any moment

        to collapse

or red-hot iron   hammered into shape
aware that

      as we cool

        we harden.

by ANDREW PHILIP, from 'The Ambulance Box',
Salt Publications 2009, used with permission

Morning Prayer

Help me listen
to Your voice of smoke
and make me obstinate
before the solid soundbite.
Teach me when to stand
rigid as a rock
and when to give way
like a stone to a stream.
Against the hard hearts,
steely eyes and flint heads.
Make me adamant
in choosing the way of Jesus

on the cross, resolute
in flesh and blood.
AMEN

Evening Prayer

When I became weary of empathy,
when I agreed with the greedy,
when I dreamed without wisdom,
when I acted without thought,
when I prayed without love,
forgive me;
may my heart burn
like Moses' bush, unconsumed
and unconsuming;
may I trust in the bright strength
of Your compassion.
AMEN

Scripture Readings

> Ezekiel 3:1–11   *God's Words*
> Luke 24:13–35   *The Road to Emmaus*

Blessing

> Let tomorrow's storm
> carry hope.
> Let tomorrow's story
> renew faith.
> Let tomorrow's void
> fill with love.
> AMEN

PRAYER NOTES

PRAYER NOTES

VESSELS – *LANDSCAPE*

The stone on the well's mouth was large, and when all the flocks were gathered there, the shepherds would roll the stone from the mouth of the well and water the sheep.

~ Genesis 29:2b–3a ~

Meditation

I imagine the scene in Haran:
uncultivated land,
fit for grazing not feasting
and gathered round the well
thirsty sheep and shepherds.

Scarce, precious, vital
water
protected
from pollution or evaporation
by a stone.

And when the time is right,
they drink
and they live.

I see the scene in Asia or Africa:
uncultivated land,
fit for grazing not feasting
and gathered round the murky pool
thirsty animals and people.

Scarce, precious, vital
water
unprotected
from pollution or evaporation
because there's not even a bloody well
never mind a stone.

And because there is no right time,
they drink
and they die.

Morning Prayer

Dear God,
if all these thousands of years ago
we knew how to use stones
to line and protect water wells
then how come today –
with all our superior knowledge
not only about water storage,
plumbing and sanitation
but also about the plight of neighbours
on the other side of the world
there are still billions dying
because they have no
clean water?

How come Lord?
And what can I do about it?
Let me think on that today.

Evening Prayer

I thank You Lord for the water
that I have used this day.
I would be hard pushed
to account for every drop
for it was not hard earned.
Forgive my excess.

Bless babies, children and adults
who have no easy access to clean water.
Bless the work and workers
of Water Aid, Oxfam, Christian Aid
and all the charities and organisations
that enable life-giving water projects.

I promise God,
I will do what I can. AMEN

Scripture Readings

| Genesis 29:1–12 | *The stone that sealed the well* |
| John 4:1–45 | *The woman at the well* |

Blessing

May the Shepherd lead you beside still waters.
May the Shepherd restore your soul.
May the Shepherd send you out to tend His flock.

VESSELS – ARCHITECTURE

Now standing there were six stone water-jars …
each holding twenty or thirty gallons.

~ John 2:6 ~

Meditation

Hewn from the rock,
hammered and chiselled,
hollowed and smoothed
there they stood
the stone water jars.

And all around
singing and dancing,
eating and drinking
as people rejoiced until …
it seemed happiness might run out.

And the hour had come
for Jesus to turn water
into the choicest wine.

Hewn from the rock,
hammered and chiselled,
hollowed and smoothed,
there they stood
the containers of miracle.

Morning Prayer

Lord Jesus,
if I am standing there
beside brothers or sisters
who do not sing but wail,
who do not dance but stagger,
who do not eat but starve,
who do not drink but thirst
and happiness
seems to have run out …

then please,
hammer and chisel me,
hollow and smooth me,
that I might be a container for You,
of even a half-gallon miracle. AMEN

Evening Prayer

Dearest Lord,
You saved the greatest miracle to the end
when cross became winepress
and You turned Yourself
into the new wine of heaven.

Thank You for every sip I have
at Your communion table.
And thank You for the invitation.

Thank You for the cup I hope to drink
at the eternal feast of life.
And thank You for the promise.

Thank You Lord for the true blessed happiness
that cannot run out
because Your love,
Your Spirit,
Your wine
are infinite.

Scripture Readings

Exodus 17:1–7   *Water from the rock*
John 2:1–11   *The wedding at Cana*

Blessing

May your good works give glory
to the Rock from which you are hewn.
May you encounter miracle
in the ordinary and the extraordinary.
And may every cup you drink
be filled with blessing and hope. AMEN

VESSELS – *PEOPLE*

A woman came to him with an alabaster jar of very costly
ointment and she poured it on his head as he sat at the table.

~ Matthew 26:7 ~

Meditation

A gleam of alabaster
symbol of purity and great honour,
in the hands of a woman
symbol of dirtiness and disgrace.

Scorn is poured over her
as the seal is broken open
and from its holy container
precious perfumed oil
spills out over Jesus' head.

What extravagance!
What prodigality of love!

An anointing
for a rite of passage
unites their spirits
and the fragrance of her faith
fills the room.

A gleam of translucent skin
as she turns
and leaves
her job well done.

Morning Prayer

Loving God,
bless all that I contain
for I know
that it does not all
smell sweet.

May what I pour over others
be the oil that calms troubled waters,
be the milk of human kindness,

be the faith that needs no words,
be the love that costs the giver.

And when I am spent
fill me again
with the perfume of Christ

And if what I pour out
is bitter and rank, then cleanse me Lord,
and anoint me with Your forgiveness. Amen

Evening Prayer

For those today
who poured themselves out for others
thank You, Lord.

For those today
who are the poor still with us
may they know Your blessing,
and may I, Your rich,
ask Your and their forgiveness.

For those today,
who kept themselves to themselves
break the seal, Lord,
unstop their goodness
and give them the confidence
to share their love, their all. Amen

Scripture Readings

1 Samuel 10:1–2	*With oil from a phial Samuel anoints Saul*
Matthew 26:6–13	*From an alabaster jar, Jesus is anointed*

Blessing

May God anoint you with blessings to spare;
may Christ call you to missions of care;
may the Spirit fill you with love to share. Amen

PRAYER NOTES

MEMORIALS – *LANDSCAPE*

So these stones shall be to the Israelites a memorial forever

~ Joshua 4:7c ~

Meditation

I fight against the cold of winter's breath
as I make my way through rows of crosses
towards the memorial wall:
a massive monolith to man's massacre of man.

The names of
our glorious dead –
too numerous to count or contemplate,
send shivers down my spine.

I turn to face the landscape bleak,
with crimson stains of poppy streaks –
this land as much a testament to these
as any stones.

I turn again, and touch the wall,
to find it strangely warm beneath my fingers.
These aren't just names, but sons and husbands,
who gave their all – that I can live.

I leave much warmer in my heart and mind
touched by this memorial to humankind.

Morning Prayer

Eternal God,
our souls struggle with all the
continuing acts of violence in our world.

Yet in the face of such inhumanity
we believe in Your promise of a better world
and know that we must be the first to change
if we wish to see Your Kingdom come.

May we come to see
that peace is not merely a distant goal we seek
but a means by which we arrive at that goal,

and that justice is not just about the outcome of events
but the working out of life in its entirety.

Help us this day to be advocates for peace
and agents of hope in our world. AMEN

Evening Prayer

Lord God of Love,
we remember with heart-felt gratitude
all those whose memories we cherish
and those whose names we will never know,
who have given of themselves
as peacemakers and peacekeepers
to keep our world secure and free.

Help us to use that freedom
as a fitting memorial to their sacrifices
and as a positive legacy for those
who are yet to come. AMEN

Scripture Readings

> Joshua 4:1–9   *Israel crosses the Jordan*
> John 5:25–29   *Jesus' authority over the dead*

Blessing

> Those who look to the Lord will win new strength,
> they will soar as on eagles' wings;
> they will run and not feel faint,
> march on and not grow weary. AMEN

MEMORIALS – *ARCHITECTURE*

This is my body ... given for you. Do this in remembrance of me.

~ Luke 22:19b ~

Meditation

A table made from stone.
Formed from the earth,
quarried by machine,
carved by hand,
fashioned for human function.

Its strength and beauty measured not
in weight, design, or price,
but in its value as
a place of welcome,
a symbol of grace,
a sign of hope,
a token of holiness
and a repository for ritual.

This is the place where earth touches heaven
and heaven touches earth.

For engraved upon its front:
'Do this in memory of me'.

Morning Prayer

Help me to remember You Lord
in the ritual of each day.
In my waking,
in my working,
in my respite
and my recreation.

Remind me of Your presence
whenever I break bread,
wherever I lift a cup
and whenever I share words with others.

May Your love flow through the liturgy of my life
allowing me to embrace the holiness of each moment
and the blessings of each day. AMEN

Evening Prayer

Come visit the sacred space within me, O God.
Come and sanctify my soul with Your presence.

I lay before You
all that has weighed heavy in my heart today
and ask that You help me bear what I must carry
and discard what I need to let go.

I place into Your presence
the tasks and challenges
that I know tomorrow will bring
and ask that You bless them with Your presence
and grace me with Your company.

Come visit the sacred space within me, O God.
Come and sanctify my soul with Your presence. AMEN

Scripture Readings

Luke 22:1–23   *The Lord's Supper*
Psalm 43   *A prayer to God in times of trouble*

Blessing

God's power to guide me,
God's might to uphold me,
God's eyes to watch over me;
God's ear to hear me,
God's word to give me speech,
God's hand to guard me,
God's way to lie before me,
God's shield to shelter me,
God's host to secure me. AMEN

First Millennium – BRIGID OF GAEL

MEMORIALS – *PEOPLE*

Then Jesus told them plainly, 'Lazarus is dead'

~ John 11:14 ~

Meditation

Will I be remembered when time passes
and distant memories fade?

Will there be a memorial to my life
to the contributions that I made?

Or will my marker lie unnoticed
in some untended graveyard
and my inscription fade away
in some memorial book?

But for God
today, and every day,
is inscribed by my presence
and each and every moment
marked as a treasured memory.
Celebrated,
cherished
and never forgotten.

Morning Prayer

Lord God of both the living and the dead,
I know that I am mortal
and one day I must die,
but help me to live my life before I do.

Help me to measure my life as You do –
to see myself as that unique element of creation
made in Your image
and held in Your immortal memory.

Help me to recognise my achievements;
to see the legacies of love I leave in the lives of others
and the difference that my life makes to those who love me.
Help me to embrace the opportunities of life

that You send my way,
and to celebrate the lives of others
that they may know their value too. AMEN

Evening Prayer

Everlasting God,
You shepherd the stars across the night skies
and companion the course of humanity.

Yet as small and as fleeting as I am
You make a place in Your heart
to comfort and to keep me.

Send Your blessings upon all those I love this day
that they too may feel Your presence in their lives
and seek Your love to guide them in their hearts. AMEN

Scripture Readings

John 11   *Jesus raises Lazarus to life*
Matthew 27:57–61   *Jesus is laid in the tomb*

Blessing

God be with me
In life
In death
In life after death.
AMEN

PRAYER NOTES

PRAYER NOTES

ROYAL PRIESTHOOD

For when there is a change in the priesthood,
there is necessarily a change in the law as well.

~ Hebrews 7:12 ~

Meditation

A group whose primary interest is in its
non-members.
A group whose idea of itself
was turned inside out by one servant.
A group whose executive
is every member, every person,
everyone who loves.
Jesus broke down the walls of the club,
made its meeting place the world.
He took the laws that had sheltered,
laws which had been a protecting temple
and blew them open with the single word:
love.
A priesthood of the people.

I am a priest,
I am the church in the world,
spreading the kingly, holy presence,
wherever I go –
how can I begin?

Morning Prayer

Lord of transformation,
You made the world when it was new,
and then You made the world anew.
You wrote a new law.
You made a new priesthood.
You took our actions and declared them to be holy,
our every day, our dressing, our talking,
our going, our coming, our making,
our breaking – royal, holy.
You gave each of us the responsibility,
the privilege of priesthood,
and our parishioners are nothing less

than the whole world.
Through my acts today,
let me serve You with the same,
honourable, priestly service,
with which You served Your apostles –
caring, washing, feeding,
and saving.
AMEN

Evening Prayer

As I prepare for sleep,
I consider the people I have served in my life.
I consider how I have served them,
with words, or thoughts, or actions.
I remember, Lord, that I was serving You
in them.
I remember, Lord, that You served me.
It is through service that our priesthood is strong;
it is through service that our souls were saved;
it is through service that the earth will be flooded with
joy, peace, forbearance, kindness,
self-control, goodness, faithfulness,
gentleness and love.

Scripture Readings

Hebrews 7:11–12   *Another priest*
Revelations 5:6–10   *The sacrifice of the lamb*

Blessing

May the Lord bless you;
may you bless those you meet,
may you be blessed in turn by
family, friends, and strangers,
in a solid ring of God's love,
in Jesus name. AMEN

PRAYER NOTES

PRAYER NOTES

GOD'S PEOPLE

Above all, clothe yourselves with love,
which binds everything together in perfect harmony.

~ Colossians 3:14 ~

Meditation

In Brazil
there are seventeen different adjectives to describe skin
colour.
That could be the kaleidoscope of God's diversity.

But it could also be the names that separate and filter.

Where we move from poetry to packaging
and start to create boxes in which to put ourselves
and others,
there are so many names that we call ourselves
and others,
so many tidy little ways by which we find our niche.

We wear our titles out with pride,
yet we also label and condemn.

We don't need colours or creed,
sexuality or superiority,
denominations or dogma,
gender or gravitas,
to define who we are.

All we need
is to be God's people.
All we need
is to clothe ourselves in love.
All we need
is to be bound in perfect harmony.

That's the joy of God
and of God's people.

Morning Prayer

As the shards of dawn's light filters through the morning
let me be awake and alive

to all of God's creation.
Let me dance with joy in all that You have given me
and in all the people that I meet this day.
Lead me away from the slavery of prejudice
and into the joyous freedom of unconditional love.

For we are all God's people.
Halleluyah! Praise the Lord!
AMEN

Evening Prayer

As my body relaxes into the air of the night
let me cast my mind back in prayer.
Let me remember all the people I met today.
Let me remember the people who escaped my notice.
Let me see the joys and the sorrows.
Let me understand the middle of the muddle of life.
For all of God's people
I give You thanks.

For we are all God's people.
Halleluyah! Praise the Lord!
AMEN

Scripture Readings

Isaiah 56:6–8	*The house of prayer for all people*
1 Corinthians 12:12–30	*All one body*

Blessing

Praise God from whom all blessings flow

James 1:17

Praise Him all creatures here below

Psalm 145:21

Praise Him above, ye heav'nly host

Revelation 5:11–14

Praise Father, Son, and Holy Ghost

Matthew 28:19

PRAYER NOTES

PRAYER NOTES

Prayer Activities

A stone is engraved with geological and historical memories

ANDY GOLDSWORTHY
(British sculptor, photographer and environmentalist)

Find a rock or stone that is in its natural state –
unprocessed in any way by human hand.
You may find one in or on the soil somewhere or on a beach.
You may have one you keep in your home or garden.

Study it, using any combination of sight, touch and smell.
In your imagination, create the story of the stone or rock.

How did it get to where you found it today?

Where, how and when might it have come into existence?

What might have been the life markings on its journey?

Imagine the rock or stone as a metaphor for yourself.

How did you get to where you find yourself today?

Where, how and when did you start life?

What have been the life markings on your journey –
of relationships, of learning, of faith, of achievements, of
failures, of risk-taking, of gains, of losses?

Whose names are engraved on your heart?

Remember always –

as a living stone of Christ,
you are engraved with theological and historical memories:
God loves you enough to lay down His life for you
and you are part of God's evolving story.

Give thanks.

What you leave behind
is not what is engraved in stone monuments,
but what is woven into the lives of others.

PERICLES
(Greek statesman, orator and general of Athens
during the Golden Age, who fostered democracy,
literature, art and freedom of expression)

Imagine all these different colours of thread going out from your life to be woven into the lives of others:

green, red, blue, yellow, pink, black, white,
purple, orange, brown.

What do each of these colours represent?

How many family members or friends can you name
who have your threads woven into the fabric of their lives?

Other than family or friends, are there others whose lives
you have influenced through your work or through
a particularly meaningful chance encounter?

Pray for each person you have named.

What would you like your legacy to be –
to your nearest and dearest,
to your friends,
to the world?

Pray about that legacy
and live towards it today and tomorrow ...

God has given us a legacy through Jesus Christ.
Pray about that legacy
and be assured of it today and tomorrow ...

Prayer Activity 3

In the West, there has always been an attempt
to try to make the religious building,
whether it's Medieval or Renaissance Church,
an eternal object for the celebration of God.
The material chosen whether stone, brick or concrete,
is meant to eternally preserve what is inside.

TADAO ANDO
(self-taught Japanese architect who emphasises
simplicity in his design believing that architecture
can change society)

If you are able, go for a walk or tour
around your neighbourhood or community
to look at all the religious buildings.

Some may be very old.
Some may be modern.
Pray for the people who use each of these buildings.

Now reflect on what these buildings are used for today.
Most may be used for their original purpose.
One or two might now be private homes or restaurants
or other commercial premises.

Does this offend you?
These buildings were erected to the glory of God
but it is those who worship within them
and journey out from them in mission and discipleship
who are the living stones.

Now accept a challenge.
Think or write a description of what
a church, the body of Christ, means to you.
You might like to do this in a group.

Now design a space, a 'temple of God',
that reflects your idea of what a church should be like inside
and what it should communicate to the outside world.

Compare your design to a familiar church.
Is the familiar church fit for purpose?
Are we in danger of 'worshipping stocks
and stones' as did our ancestors?
Pray on this.

The gods had condemned Sisyphus
to ceaselessly rolling a rock to the top of a mountain,
whence the stone would fall back of its own weight.
They had thought with some reason
that there is no more dreadful punishment
than futile and hopeless labour.

ALBERT CAMUS
(French Nobel prize winning author, journalist and philosopher)

Find a stone or pebble and cup it in your open palms.
Think about all the things that are worrying you just now.
Think through them each in detail while focusing on the stone.
When you are finished,
close your palms over the stone for a second
and then put it somewhere where you will carry it about
for a day or so – maybe a pocket, or a hand bag.

When you come across it or remember it during the day,
think about what you carry with you.

When you are ready, take a quiet moment to sit with your stone,
clasp all the worries that you have,
and offer them up to God.

Ask Him to lift those worries from you.

Lay down the stone somewhere you choose,
maybe your garden, maybe out and about,
maybe somewhere in your house.

Feel the release of letting go.
Talk to God about how you feel.

The least movement is of importance to all nature.
The entire ocean is affected by a pebble.

BLAISE PASCAL
(French mathematician, physicist, inventor,
writer and Christian philosopher)

Take a handful of pebbles of different sizes.
Sort them in size,
from the smallest to the largest, or vice versa.
You may want to number them.

As you look at them, one by one,
pray from the smallest to the largest,

first for small, intimate things,
then, moving outwards,
increase the circle of your prayers.

(Or pray from the largest to the smallest, depending
on the way you organised the stones.)

On some days you may want to concentrate
on one or other of the stones; on other days you may
want to pray through all sizes, whichever way round.
You may want to keep the stones where you can see them,
so that your prayers will always be present
in your mind and heart.

Prayer Activity 6

Every charitable act is a stepping stone towards heaven.

Henry Ward Beecher
*(American Congregationalist clergyman,
social reformer and speaker,
known for his support of the abolition of slavery)*

As of September 2014, there were 167,097 registered charities in the United Kingdom (figures from those published by UK Government's Charity Commission). By the time you read this some of these charities will have folded and some new ones will have come into existence.

What are your most favoured charities? Why?
Pray for them – those they assist and those who work or volunteer for them.

We live in an age of charity shops, food banks and voluntary organisations on which many people now depend.

Which charity shops do you pass most regularly?
Which voluntary organisations are most active in the community in which you live?

Where is your nearest food bank?
How could you support or become more involved in any of the above?

Pray for the children, families and individuals in your local community who most depend on social services and local voluntary organisations to help them to help themselves.

Pray for all who experience any form of deprivation – financial, educational or social.

Prayer Activity 7

Too long a sacrifice can make a stone of the heart.

W. B. YEATS
*(Irish poet and one of the foremost figures
of 20th-century literature)*

Jesus is our example of the ultimate,
all-time sacrifice on the Cross.

Think of people you know who have
'laid down their lives for a friend' (John 15:13).
It may be someone who is caring for a parent, a partner,
a child, a relative or a friend.
Pray for them and the ones they care for.

Caring full-time is all demanding.
Most people who do this will say that it is not a sacrifice
because it is done in love so it is an offering.

Yet even in love,
such complete giving of self over a long period of time
may become so onerous, so all consuming,
so emotionally draining,
that we become hardened or even 'deadened'
because it is the only way to cope.

Can you identify with this?

Is there a carer close to you
who needs your tender loving care at this time?

Think how often we ask about the person who is being
cared for
and fail to ask the carer how she or he is.

Pray for all the children who are full-time carers.

Pray for all the carers who are, at this time,
having to make the decision
about putting their loved one into full-time professional
care
because they can no longer cope at home.

Always remember,
Jesus said, 'Love your neighbour as yourself' (Matt. 22:39).
Even in loving sacrifice we still have to love ourselves.

Even in sacrifice we need friends just as Jesus wanted his friends to watch with him while he prayed in the garden (Mark 14:32–42).

Prayer Activity 8

Love doesn't just sit there like a stone;
it has to be made, like bread,
remade all the time, made new.

URSULA K. LE GUIN
(American author of novels,
children's books and short stories)

Reflect on the above quote.

What does it mean to you?

In the Lord's Prayer, we ask God to 'give us this day
our daily bread' (Matt. 6:11) – not tomorrow's, not next
week's
or month's or year's
but just sufficient for our true need this very day.

What does this say to us about love?
Are we also praying, implicitly,
'give us this day our daily love'?

Who gives you love daily?
Remember not only those physically present to you
but also those who send their love
from somewhere here or from heaven.
Never forget that God loves you every moment of every
day.
Pray for those who love you daily and those whom you
love.

Jesus used breaking and sharing bread at the last supper
to show His disciples how His body
would be broken open in love for them (1 Cor. 11:23–24).
He asked them to remember Him every time they broke
bread.

Just as bread is consumed and needs made anew
so too every kiss, every hug, every genuine expression
of love or forgiveness
breaks open the giver and feeds the soul of the receiver.
Expressions of love are made new each day.

Love is both a noun and a living verb.

God the Noun is the Rock of our salvation.
Jesus the Living Verb is the means.
Pray on this.

The observer, when he seems to himself to be observing a stone,
is really, if physics is to be believed,
observing the effects of the stone upon himself.

BERTRAND RUSSELL
(British philosopher, logician, mathematician,
historian, social critic and political activist)

To what extent do we view all experiences in life
and all people
in terms of how they affect our being and well-being?

Reflect on this.

Take a stone or gemstone.
Study it.
Do you find it beautiful? Does it shine?
Is it pleasingly smooth or are there sharp, rough edges?
Does it seem warm or cold?

Is this how we study people?

Can we also relate the analogy to church?
When we think about our fellow worshippers
or what happens in church especially in times of change,
are we sometimes guilty of thinking
only of the effect upon ourselves?

Pray for the people you find ugly or dull or sharp,
or scary or distasteful.
Admit to God your feelings towards them,
pray for a change of heart and try to view them differently.

Pray for the church – for those who fear change
and for the future generations who will inherit
either our faithful risk-taking or our faith-lacking
cowardice.

Dripping water hollows out stone, not by force,
but through persistence.

OVID
(Ancient Roman poet
best known for his 'Metamorphoses')

St Paul had his road to Damascus experience
when the Lord spoke to him and the stone-hearted man
who was then named Saul was destroyed.
After three days in a tomb of blindness,
the disciple named Ananias laid hands on him
and he received the Holy Spirit.
Saul was resurrected as Paul, the apostle.

For some, faith does come in a dramatic life-changing
experience.
But for many, our knowledge about God
and our relationship with God through Jesus
is more of a 'drip-feed' process.

Reflect on how you have come,
and are coming, to know God more closely.
Who and what have been your influences?
Give thanks for them.

Getting to the inside,
to the heart of someone we love can mean persistence –
persistence of love,
persistence of patience,
persistence of gentleness,
persistence of presence.
God persists with each of us.

Is there someone for whom you are the persistent drip
of living water?
Pray for that person.
Pray that you never give up.

Stone walls do not a prison make
nor iron bars a cage.

RICHARD LOVELACE
(17th-century English poet)

Give thanks for the living stones such as
Dietrich Bonhoeffer
and
Nelson Mandela
whose bodies were imprisoned
but whose souls, minds and hearts remained liberated
to praise God, act justly, walk humbly and love tenderly.

Can you think of other examples of 'living stones?
Give thanks for the freedoms which you appreciate.

Pray for men, women and children who have been trafficked
to become enslaved in the sex, building or hospitality trade,
or imprisoned in domestic servitude
or made to carry out street crimes.

Log on to
www.scotland.police.uk/keep-safe/advice-for-victims-of-crime/human-trafficking/potential-signs-of-human-trafficking/
or www.stopthetraffik.org
to find out what you can do as an individual to fight trafficking.

Pray for all who are in prison –
those who are there justly and unjustly –
and for their families
and for all who work in prisons
or make legislation regarding prisons.

Reflect on how the church can support those who
have come out of prison
and are trying to integrate back into the local community.

Every block of stone has a statue inside it
and it is the task of the sculptor to discover it.

MICHELANGELO
(Italian painter, sculptor, poet architect and engineer)

Remembering the theme of this book is 'Living Stones',
reflect on the quote above.

God is our Sculptor.
It is God's task to find the statue within us.
It is God's task to hollow, to shape, to mould.

Look in a mirror.
Do you see a living statue sculpted by God?
Do you see the image of Christ reflected back to you?

Michelangelo's most famous sculpture is the gleaming
white
marble statue of David in Florence. The figure stands
naked and
armed only with his sling, his small rock, his faith and his
courage
ready to take on the giant Goliath (1 Sam. 17).

Have you the faith to look in the mirror
and stand naked before yourself,
clothed only in Christ and armed with His love? (Gal. 3:27)
Pray about this.

Do you think God will finish 'your statue' in this life-time
or will you still be a 'work in progress'
till your last day on earth?
Reflect on this.

To what extent
does God use us to help to sculpt others
to reveal the true statue within?

Give thanks for those who have been God's instruments
of sculpture in your life.

Acknowledgements

Pray Now: Living Stones was prepared by members of the Pray Now Writing Group: Adam Dillon, Peggy Ewart-Roberts, Carol Ford, Mark Foster, Tina Kemp, Ishbel McFarlane, Rob A. McKenzie, and MaryAnn Rennie.

Daily headline Scripture quotations are taken from the New Revised Standard Version, © 1989 Division of Christian Education of the National Council of Churches of Christ in the United States of America, published by Oxford University Press.

With special thanks to Robert McQuistan and Lynn Hall for their work in preparing the final manuscript.